Colours o

Also by Adrian Plass
and available from HarperCollins*Publishers*:

A Year at St Yorick's
Adrian Plass Classics
An Alien at St Wilfred's
Cabbages for the King
Clearing Away the Rubbish
Father to the Man and Other Stories
Stress Family Robinson
Stress Family Robinson 2: The Birthday Party
The Final Boundary
The Growing Up Pains of Adrian Plass
The Horizontal Epistles of Andromeda Veal
The Sacred Diary of Adrian Plass aged 37¾
The Sacred Diary of Adrian Plass aged 45¾
The Theatrical Tapes of Leonard Thynn
The Visit
Why I Follow Jesus

Colours of Survival

Discovering Hope in Bangladesh

Adrian and Bridget Plass

Marshall Pickering
An Imprint of HarperCollins*Publishers*

Marshall Pickering is an Imprint of
HarperCollins*Religious*
part of HarperCollins*Publishers*
77–85 Fulham Palace Road, London W6 8JB
www.christian-publishing.com

First published in Great Britain in 2000
by HarperCollins*Publishers*

1 3 5 7 9 10 8 6 4 2

Illustrations by Ben Ecclestone

Taken by Sanjay Sojwal and Peter Scott

A catalogue record for this book is
available from the British Library

ISBN 0 551 03251 0

Printed and bound in Great Britain by
Omnia Books Ltd, Glasgow

He raises the poor from the dust and lifts the needy from the ash heap.

Psalm 113: 7–8

The words we have written are dedicated,
with our love, to Shahnaj Begum.

• Contents •

• Introduction •

A: This book is the story of a journey made by my wife, Bridget, and myself to Bangladesh in the first month of the first year of the new millennium. It is certainly not a complete account of that journey because, although we were there for only two weeks, the little hard-backed, brown notebooks we took with us, one marked A for Adrian, the other marked B for Bridget (sweet, isn't it?) are absolutely stuffed with impressions, memories, thoughts and descriptions. We would need to write three or four books to get it all in. You'll be able to tell which of us has written each section, incidentally, by looking for the A or the B near the top of the piece. We don't waste ideas once we've had them, I can tell you!

The project was initiated and planned by an organization called World Vision. This is how they describe themselves:

> *World Vision is an international development and humanitarian agency dedicated to the relief of suffering and improving the quality of life of the world's poorest people. We are a Christian organization. Our commitment is founded on our belief in Jesus Christ whose life demonstrated compassion and service to all.*

The plan was that we would fly to Dhaka, the capital, meet the little girl we have sponsored through World Vision for the last five years, and visit a variety of projects in different parts of the country. On our return we would write a book about our experiences and host a national tour to raise awareness of third world needs in general and child sponsorship in particular.

For those concerned that the exercise might have absorbed cash that would otherwise have been used to relieve poverty, it's worth recording that neither Bridget nor I are employed by World Vision in any capacity, and that all expenses involved in our saga were taken from money paid by the publisher, HarperCollins, in the form of advance royalties on this book. All future royalties earned by the book will be donated to World Vision.

This unattached brief caused us to approach the whole thing with considerable trepidation. What if we discovered that World Vision workers were a load of con-artists using donations from the west to finance international crime? What if we found it all very uninspiring and had to give the money back? What if we became third world bores and drove everyone mad in England afterwards by going on and on about the starving millions? What if we really loathed our sponsor child when we met her? What if she hated us? What if there was nothing funny in Bangladesh? What if we didn't understand how to flush the toilets? What if – oh, lots of things.

So, how *did* we get on? Well, that's what the book is about – including the toilets – so please read it.

Before we begin, though, we would like to thank a whole host of World Vision workers, both in the United Kingdom and in Bangladesh, who worked very, very hard to make our trip useful and enjoyable. It was a great joy to encounter so many Christian brothers and sisters at World Vision headquarters in Dhaka, and at other offices around the country. I never cease to be amazed and reassured by the bond that exists between genuine followers of Jesus wherever they meet in the world. To all these new friends in Bangladesh, we want to say how very much we valued our time with you. Thank you all for your loving concern. We shall not forget you.

Thanks also to our children for lending us to another nation for a fortnight.

Most of all we thank Jesus, who loves the poor of Bangladesh, and meets them there every day through the dedicated hands and feet and voices of his followers.

• BEFORE •

Aids and kidnap – early shocks

A: 'You will be taking an Aids kit just like this.'

I gazed in dumb horror at the green, rectangular zipped-up case lying on the table in front of me. This nice lady who was responsible for the first phase of our briefing at the headquarters of World Vision in Milton Keynes, had produced and identified this bizarre piece of equipment as though it was a cup of tea or a biscuit.

What in the name of something-or-other did these people think we were planning to do when we got to Bangladesh? For one wild, insane moment I wondered if protocol on this trip demanded some kind of inappropriate sexual contact with – no, no, don't be so *stupid*! Listen to what the nice lady's saying ...

'You can't be at all sure that things like syringes are going to be clean in the sort of areas you're going to, so, if you were to be injured or something, you'd be well prepared with this little kit, wouldn't you?'

'Well, yes, of course – yes, I see that.'

Of course I saw that. Huh! Of course I did. Phew! Fancy me being so silly. Fancy me thinking—

'And these are your kidnap forms.'

'These are our ...'

'Your kidnap forms. We ask you to sign these so that in the event of you being kidnapped we won't be obligated to pay a ransom. That wouldn't be what we wanted at all, would it?'

'No, no, of course not,' I gurgled, 'no, if we were kidnapped we, er, certainly wouldn't want that.'

My strangled laughter trailed away as a mental picture formed of Bridget and me chained up in some terrorist dungeon, any hope of ransom signed away long ago in Milton Keynes, injured and awaiting imminent death because our Aids kit had been stolen by our kidnappers. What on earth had we let ourselves in for?

Somewhat cheered by having it explained to us that these things were part of routine procedure for all those travelling to such parts of the world (obviously it would be disastrous for World Vision to be thought a soft touch for terrorists all over the world), we continued with our other briefing sessions, returning at the end of the day to our home in Hailsham. Later, we met with Peter Scott, Church Relations Officer for World Vision UK, in a London restaurant for further discussions about the trip. There we were duly presented with our very own zipped-up green case. This was fine until the time came to leave. I stood up and was just starting to move away from the table, when Peter called out in a fairly loud voice, 'Oh, Adrian, you've forgotten your Aids kit!'

A fascinated silence fell among those seated at the tables near to ours. Rightly or wrongly, everything in me wanted, in classic Basil Fawlty style, to formally address the assembled clientele on the subject of my Aids kit, and its contingent function within the context of our forthcoming trip.

But I didn't. I grabbed my green case and I disappeared from that place as if pursued by kidnappers, forgiving Peter pungently as I went.

BEFORE

How it began

A: Nagging guilt and vague sympathy, those are the things that prodded Bridget and me into sponsoring a child in the first place. Pathetic, isn't it? But never mind. We did it. And now we know it's more than a good idea. It's a vital one.

Five years after we started our sponsorship of Shahnaj Begum, a little girl living in the slums of Bangladesh, it was suggested by Peter Scott that we might fly out to Dhaka, capital city of one of the poorest countries in the world, to meet Shahnaj and, as I explained in the introduction, to collect material for a book about our experiences. Bridget will speak for herself, but I must be honest and confess that our sponsor child had very little reality in my mind at that point. Indeed, I was oppressed, on the rare occasions when I thought about it at all, by feelings of guilt about my failure to take any real trouble or care over the responsibility that we had taken on. Yes, the money went out regularly because it was on a standing order from the bank, but that, by and large, was that.

Now we were going to spend two weeks in Bangladesh. We would meet Shahnaj. The country she lived in and she herself were going to become real. I don't think either of us really understood what that would mean.

Didn't really want to meet her ...

B: What I am about to say is not easy for me. You see, I didn't really want to meet my sponsor child.

From the moment the idea was mooted that Adrian and I should go to Bangladesh I was aware of a growing sense of impending danger. Oh, I don't mean that I was concerned for our personal physical safety. For some reason that sort of thing has never worried me unduly. Nor was I reluctant to take on the responsibility and time commitment that I was immediately aware the project would involve. On the contrary, that felt like an enormous privilege. No, the danger that threatened was in the area of my emotional safety. I was born with an exceptionally thin skin, and from small childhood I have had to develop strategies to help me survive in an emotionally charged world.

One of my most effective strategies has been to fasten a veil firmly in place over the appalling pictures the media constantly presents of those whose living conditions I am incapable of changing, to avoid the faces of the children I could not help. The decision to sponsor a child, when it came, was in response to an advertising campaign which majored on the fact that you may not be able to save the world from suffering, but you could make a difference to the life of one small struggling human being. It was an idea that appealed to both Adrian and me. Having been involved for years in residential social work we had frequently had to answer to the accusation that we should be more politically involved, so that we could help to bring about reforms in our society which would render much of our work unnecessary.

Our reply had tended to be, 'Well, you get on with sorting out how to improve the perches, and in the meantime we'll look after the sparrows that have already fallen.'

I recall the day we received the first photo of Shahnaj. I remember peering into the passport-sized photo of a brown-eyed, endearingly anxious little girl and trying to bring her alive in my mind. I couldn't. The veil was too securely in place. I just couldn't afford for her to be too real. The pain of acknowledging her level of hardship as opposed to the comparative luxury my own four children had experienced might swamp me. For five years I had thought with a small degree of relief that at least I was doing something, albeit something meagre, to help someone somewhere. I had enjoyed sending the cards and tiny gifts we were encouraged to send at birthdays and Christmas, but in my heart I had determinedly remained uninvolved. And now …?

Facts, fears and flying

B: Our flight has proved to be the normal club-sandwich affair of films, food and frustration at not being able to sleep, but now we have left Delhi for the last lap of the journey, and I have been able to secure a seat next to the window. I lean my face against it, staring down and willing my eyes to penetrate the soft meringue-like peaks of cloud which densely cover whatever mysteries lie beneath.

I know lots of facts. I've spent most of the journey rereading the material given by World Vision to help us orientate ourselves with Bangladesh. I know about the whole country being basically a delta of some of the mightiest rivers of the world, the Ganges, Brahmaputra and Jumuna. I know that 90 per cent of the country is composed of alluvial plains less than ten metres above sea level. I've been reminded of the many television programmes I've seen over the years documenting the tragedies of the 1971 famine, the '88 and '98 floods and the '91 cyclone. I even know by heart some of the appalling statistics which cause Bangladesh to be labelled the fifth poorest country in the world.

The history has admittedly been a bit more of a challenge, and after again ploughing through the thick mud of facts I decide to ask my learned partner what he thinks it's all about.

BRIDGET: Adrian, if you had to sum up the history of Bangladesh in just a few words, what would you say?
ADRIAN: Just a few words?
BRIDGET: Yes.
ADRIAN: Hmm ... (as if a little disappointed) You're not talking about me going into a sort of lengthy, detailed account of all the various events and their meanings – that kind of thing?
BRIDGET: (dryly) No, no, I wouldn't want to put you to that kind of trouble, darling. Just a brief synopsis will do fine.
ADRIAN: (rather vaguely for one who is supposedly having to condense such vast tracts of knowledge) Er, well, I suppose it's that bit that used to be a bit of Pakistan only cut off from the rest, but isn't any more. Er, that's about it really.

Leaving A.J.P. Taylor to doze after this masterly reconstruction of the life of a nation, I leaf through my notes and discover the following, slightly more helpful summary.

Bangladesh was part of India under British rule until that ended in 1947. After the British left the subcontinent, the land now known as Bangladesh became the eastern wing of Pakistan, or East Pakistan. Unhappy with the treatment Bengalis were receiving from Urdu-speaking West Pakistan, the leader of East Pakistan's largest political party, Sheikh Mujibur Rahman, began an independence campaign which turned into a full-scale liberation war in March 1971. The Pakistani army cracked down heavily on Bengali-speaking nationalists and much blood was shed before Bangladesh became an independent and sovereign state on December 16th, 1971.

Following independence, Bangladesh remained a parliamentary democracy until 1975 when Sheikh Mujibur Rahman was killed during a military coup. From 1975 until 1991 the country was ruled, directly or indirectly, by the armed forces. A referendum in September 1991 approved a new constitution, and Bangladesh is now once more a democracy.

With my mind clearer on the history of the country we're flying towards, documents about political structure, religion and traditions have seemed a cinch. I've even had time between the spicy chicken and rice dinners which we have been presented with at regular intervals to try to memorize some of the protocol so that I don't disgrace myself as soon as I set foot in Dhaka airport.

Did you know, for example, that, in Bangladesh, you never, never make an OK sign by putting up your thumb while the rest of your hand is clenched? Apparently it is the western equivalent of gesturing by holding up just one finger, which would hardly have the desired friendly effect.

So, on one level I am well armed with facts. On another I am aware that in a real sense I know nothing at all.

My somewhat panicky thoughts turn to my mother and father, who at the ages of eighty-four and ninety-two respectively are in the process of moving from Norfolk and buying a little bungalow over the road from us.

'It's no good, dear,' my mother had said to me on the phone only days before, 'I've read all the house details again and again but I need to see it for myself.'

Yes. I know what she means. I need to know, to see, to smell, to feel Bangladesh and I have fourteen days to do so, starting from – well, right now, judging from the sudden dip in altitude. My apprehension at meeting Shahnaj, my fears, the effort involved in solving the inevitable problems of leaving home for a fortnight are all fading. At last I am getting excited.

My initial glimpse through the thinning, wispier clouds is of a child's first painting, so random are the shapes and loops which are coming into view. Now it is a delicate tapestry of muted green, yellow and brown squares over which has been sewn a swirling pattern of shining grey satin ribbons and tiny square buttons.

As we descend further I am able to identify the ribbons as numerous brown, snaking rivers glittering in the setting sun, while the yellow and green squares are clearly just small, orderly fields made transiently beautiful by the watercolour wash of early evening. I am still very puzzled and amused by what now seem to be brown paving slabs set in concrete, but the buttons are becoming Lego-like blocks of what must be high-rise flats, and I realize that our plane is now directly over the capital city, Dhaka.

Perhaps the veil will lift.

I find to my relief that I am impatient for our adventure to begin.

• GETTING THERE •

Baggage

A: We finally landed in Bangladesh after twelve hours spent in seats that, as usual, had mysteriously halved in size since we left Heathrow. For the last couple of those hours both of us had craved good old-fashioned horizontality as a drowning man craves air. Fortunately, actually arriving in this distant foreign airport had its own built-in, enlivening excitement. First, though, there was the little matter of collecting our luggage.

Waiting for our bags to appear at Dhaka airport was as nerve-racking as it always has been everywhere else. Bridget and I have experienced the non-arrival of our luggage so often that we begin to see a special significance in the mystical truth that RECLAIM is an anagram of MIRACLE. Most of us passengers are very similar, though. You probably all do the same things as me when it comes to collecting baggage.

First of all I have to choose between pinching the last decent trolley from an elderly, handicapped, partially sighted traveller when her back is turned, or making do with the broken one that no one else wants.

Well, as a Christian you're lumbered, aren't you?

So, trying to look confident but casual, I stand with my three-wheeled trolley next to what I desperately hope is the correct carousel for my flight, throwing covert glances to left and right in the hope that I might identify someone who was definitely on the same plane as me. Ah, yes, good! That skinny, cross-eyed bloke with the yellow hair was a prisoner in the aisle seat just across from me, so I am right – or if I'm wrong then he's wrong as well, which is nowhere near as bad as being wrong on your own.

After that it's just a matter of waiting. In the other world that exists behind those thick rubber flaps over there at the end of the belt a kind of magic is about to happen. The cases and bags that I trustingly abandoned to another, less sympathetic belt years and years and miles and miles ago are about to emerge dramatically, and trundle towards my nervously expectant arms like small children released from school – I hope.

As I wait I reflect yet again on the fact that, in my heart of hearts, I don't really believe those cases travel on the plane at all. No, no, there is some process of molecular destruction and reconstitution that makes this reclaim miracle possible, rather like the process by which personnel are beamed up and down from planet to ship and vice versa on *Star Trek*. Or perhaps it's more like *The Fly*, that film in which a scientist learns how to transport items from one chamber to another, but runs into trouble when a fly gets into the despatch chamber with him, and a grotesque creature that is half man, half fly materializes at the other end. Lost in this fantasy, I imagine strange, mutant articles of luggage lurching miserably into sight and passing me dumbly on the belt. Suitcases with half a rucksack protruding grotesquely from the place where the handle should be, cloth bags that have become one gigantic zip with a minuscule container attached, ladies' overnight bags that have eviscerated themselves so that the underwear is on the outside and the leather is folded neatly away inside ...

Suddenly, with a loud thumping click and a whirring hum of

machinery the belt begins to move. All eyes fix on the rubber flaps. Nothing comes out. *Nothing* is coming out. Why is nothing coming out? Why do they tease us like this? Why have they bothered to switch on the belt if they aren't going to put any luggage on it? All the luggage must have been lost. All my luggage must have been – wait a minute, there's that crashing, dumping sound. That usually means something's going to happen. Something's coming through! Oh, Lord, just once! Just for once let it be my case that comes through first! Yes – no, it's not my case. Nor is this. Nor this. None of these are mine. Is there a God?

Illogically, I fret over the fact that the luggage I have seen so far is not even of a similar type to mine. At last a case that is a bit like mine hoves into view. I try, by an effort of the will, to make it mine, to believe that it could be mine. It's roughly the right colour. It's roughly the right size. One of my hands creeps out pathetically towards the case as it reaches the point where I'm standing. I whip it back quickly as the man next to me leans down and manfully yanks the piece of luggage that, on closer inspection, looks nothing like mine, away from the belt and on to his trolley. Oh, how I wish that I was him! Look, look, there he goes, pushing his trolley away, happy as Larry, heading for the Nothing To Declare channel.

So distracted am I by this man's good fortune that I almost miss my own delinquent case as it flies by gleefully on its way to begin the whole circuit again. I commit what must seem a deliberate assault on the person who has moved in to take the lucky man's place as, panic-stricken, I lean across him to arrest my luggage, nearly sweeping the poor fellow's legs from under him as I haul it towards me. I apologize, but it's all right. He understands. He would have done the same. He is a fellow traveller.

I make my way to the exit. I have nothing to declare either – well, perhaps just one thing: 'Thank God my luggage has arrived.'

Do you think that if Jesus had been alive today, he would have met the rich young ruler down by the luggage carousel after a long flight, and invited him to follow without waiting for his baggage to turn up? And would he have gone? Would you? Would I?

How would we have managed in Bangladesh without all our baggage?

Our bags did turn up in the end, thank goodness, and we were further relieved when we identified the familiar figure of Peter Scott, who would be spending most of the first week with us, waiting to greet us on the other side of the customs declaration point.

With Peter waited two people who were to become centrally important to us during our stay. One was the World Vision worker responsible for guest relations, whose name was Sujit Areng, and the other was Dhiman, employed by World Vision as a driver. He would be taking us wherever we needed to go for most of the following fortnight. More about both of those men later.

Dhaka at night was a fairground, bustling with chaotic life and light and noise, until our vehicle turned into the comparatively quiet side road where our guesthouse was located.

'If I wasn't a Christian,' I muttered to myself as we parked in front of the hotel, 'I would think this a very good omen indeed.'

The hotel was called 'Far Pavilions', a name which inspired me for the elevated and noble reason that there is a Bangladeshi restaurant in Edinburgh with exactly the same name, which just happens to be one of the very best in the whole of the United Kingdom ...

This book is not intended to be an advert for anybody, but if ever anyone deserved a plug, it must be the staff at Far Pavilions. From the very first moment that we stepped nervously over the threshold they looked after us superbly. I would go so far as to say that for sheer charm and warmth of hospitality you would find nothing to surpass that establishment in the whole of these islands of ours. If ever you happen to find yourself in Dhaka – drop in at Far Pavilions and spend the night. You won't regret it.

First dawn

B: It is 5.30 in the morning and we are both awake but trying desperately not to be, an experience shared by all those who have ever experienced the effects of changing time zones on their sleep patterns. We listen to the first call to prayer booming out of the darkness and silence like some monster child demanding to be fed. I doze and wake again. It is a little lighter and this time the call to prayer is accompanied by a backing group.

'Sounds like a load of ducks,' Adrian mutters.

Somewhere below in the street someone coughs and spits.

'That bloke seems to have developed the expulsion of superfluous saliva into an oral art form,' murmurs my beloved as he turns violently into sleep, taking the duvet with him.

I feel lonely and strangely displaced. We have been given a lovely apartment in the guesthouse used by World Vision for 'western' visitors. Not only does it have a huge bedroom but also a sitting room with plumpy red velvet furniture and rugs. Aware from all that I have read about the conditions in which families are surviving in the slums we are to visit, I add guilt and confusion to my bag of emotions and, for a moment, long to be at home getting my daughter Kate's packed lunch and moaning to her about not eating a proper breakfast.

Ashamed of my silliness I slide out of bed and taking my book, the latest Susan Howatch, lent to me by a friend, two digestive biscuits brought from home and a banana supplied by the hotel, go over to the window. I can see trees, a medical centre, several blocks of flats and, immediately opposite, the crumbling shell of a large building which could be on its way up or down but at the moment looks as though it has been untidily tied with twine. Closer inspection shows that it is in fact supported by bamboo scaffolding, which has a far too casual air for my liking. Everything has a strange pixillated effect because of the mosquito netting covering the window, but I can see clearly enough to discover that Adrian's ducks are in fact large black birds. They're everywhere, rocking on the banana palm leaves, dislodging the thick browny-yellow dust with which they are coated into the street below, where two small children are attempting to sweep it away from the entrance to the medical centre.

I open the window and step on to our balcony. The air is so dry it catches at my throat. It has a distinct smell which I had noticed the evening before and which I come to realize is pure pollution. Looking around at the dusty tropical foliage it all reminds me of a rather tired display of artificial tropical splendour at our local swimming pool.

Below, in the uneven concrete street two small boys with besom brooms appear to be searching among the vast piles of rubbish which decorate this area of uptown Dhaka. With animated discussion they select their treasures, putting their finds in the black dustbin bags that a tiny girl is holding open for them. A woman pads slowly up the street, a shawl hugged round her thin shoulders, reminding me that this is in fact their winter. On her head is a ridiculously vast basket containing what looks like another array of rubbish finds. It all feels rather sad and silent and I am glad to hear Adrian moving in the room behind me, hunting noisily for his comb and bemoaning the fact that, before leaving, he forgot to show Kate how to set the alarm.

Water, water everywhere – and breakfast!

A: 'Whatever you do, don't drink the water!'

So firmly had it been drummed into us that we must consume only bottled water in Bangladesh, that on that first morning and for the first couple of days of our stay I entered the spotlessly clean bathroom of our apartment in Far Pavilions as if a devil lurked in the pipes waiting to jump out and devour me. Every aspect of the self-cleansing process had to be monitored and adjusted so that wicked germs could be kept at bay.

In the shower, for instance, it was all right to let hot water run over the top of my head and down my body, but there was no question of indulging in the wild spluttering and spitting that usually concluded this stage of my ablutions. Instead, I kept my tightly closed mouth firmly, grimly pressed up against my nostrils (can you do that?) throughout the operation, eventually staggering from the shower cubicle uninfected but puce in the face and very nearly on the point of suffocation.

The germs must have danced with frustrated fury after I had been to the toilet as well. First I would wash my hands with water from a bottle, and then I would rewash them with an antiseptic lotion that Bridget had cleverly bought at Boots before we left England.

'Never mind,' the microbes no doubt said to themselves, as they rubbed their unhygienic little hands in anticipatory glee, 'we'll get him when he cleans his teeth!'

But they didn't. Oh, no! Because, you see, I used bottled water to actually clean my teeth with, bottled water to clean my toothbrush with afterwards, and bottled water to wash my hands with when I'd finished, not to mention yet another application of the good old Boots stuff just to round the whole thing off.

We didn't half get through some bottled water – and some Boots stuff.

Those first two days were all about water. I fear that, as you can tell from the above, I became something of a bad-water-avoidance bore. But here's an interesting thing. Excluding a bout of flu that I suffered from in the first week, presumably caused by an enterprising bug that must have got the travel itch and decided to bum a ride with me from England, I felt fitter in just about every possible way throughout my fortnight in Bangladesh than I had for months back home. This, I imagine, was due to a very substantial but much simpler, healthier diet, and – good clean water.

The irony of that fact is, I can assure you, not lost on me.

Our first experience of eating was interesting as well.

Breakfast at Far Pavilions, as well as giving us the chance to meet more of the charmingly attentive people who worked there, produced two major revelations about life in Bangladesh. Both were in my favour, which was good, because I think it must have been just about my turn.

The first one was to do with sugar. You see, I normally take three sugars. There, I've said it. I'll say it again. When I drink tea or coffee I like to have *three* sugars in it. Not one, not two, but three. I do not like having coffee or tea without sugar, and I do not like pretending to like having it with too little sugar, and I definitely do not like having it with that artificial sweetener stuff that claims to have no aftertaste but actually does. Nowadays, in England, when someone makes me a drink and asks if I take sugar, I say:

'Yes, three please, and no comments.'

Now, I know this sounds rather rude, and I suppose it is, but its purpose is to deflect sharp intakes of breath, incredulous, high-pitched repetitions of the word 'three', unnecessarily energetic searches through the kitchen cupboard because 'quite honestly, we hardly ever use it nowadays' and funereal shakings of the head accompanied by dismal anecdotes about local people who dropped dead yesterday morning from sugar-related illnesses before reaching their fiftieth birthdays.

So, revelation number one – in Bangladesh they make tea with sugar already in it! I am the norm. I am one of the crowd, the good old everyday crowd who have sugar in their tea because – well, come on, for goodness' sake, that's the normal thing to do. Poor old Bridget, who, rather weirdly in my view, takes no sugar in her drinks, had to have her own special pot! Put them to an awful lot of trouble, of course, but there we are. Some people are so demanding with their strange, stubborn little idiosyncrasies, aren't they?

Revelation number two was that in Bangladesh the men are served before the women. At first I couldn't believe it. Bridget is actually one of the least demanding people in the universe, and would never claim the right to any special treatment, but we were both quite taken aback by the way in which my food invariably arrived before hers, just as all my other needs were given top priority throughout our stay. As time went by we were to discover that this particular aspect of Bangladeshi society has extremely serious implications for those whom World Vision are trying to reach, but for now it just meant – well, it meant that I got my breakfast first.

I suppose, on reflection, I could have said something, but it would have been wrong to upset them, wouldn't it?

Having drunk our tea (sweetened and unsweetened), eaten our individual omelettes and consumed our toast and jam, we returned to our apartment, cleaned our teeth with bottled water, had a brief but pungent argument about less than nothing, and set off with Peter to have a look at the city of Dhaka.

• DHAKA •

The city

B: What was Dhaka actually like? A reasonable question, but one which, even after a fortnight in and around the city, I find almost impossible to answer.

There is a sense of confusion, perhaps exemplified by that first building I saw which was either being built or knocked down. Everywhere there are buildings giving the impression of somehow being held together with bits of string and lumps of cement, as inexpertly added as a child's playdough.

My thoughts go to my first sighting of human beings at work in the city. Those two small boys attempting to sweep dust and tree droppings away from the entrance to the medical building opposite our hotel with their little home-made brooms. There was absolutely no way they could succeed in their task of cleaning the street as the dust continued to fall and the trees continued to shed their load, yet still they went through the motions purely for the immediate reward of a few taka (the local currency – approximately 100 to the pound). For me these children seemed to symbolize the ineffectiveness of human endeavour in bringing about any change for the better. There is a sense of weariness and defeat in the citizens of this once beautiful city. Weariness at the sight of stewing, festering piles of garbage. Weariness at travelling on pitted, overcrowded, chaotic, polluted roads. Weariness at hearing reports of water shortages or contamination, of power abuse and violence.

Dhaka city has become one of the world's truly hopeless urban cases. Fleeing droughts, floods and starvation, people have arrived steadily from the country villages, presumably with a little hope but nothing else. As someone once wrote, 'only need is stockpiled in this already sick city'. I find it hard to believe that sixty per cent of the populace live in illegally built or substandard housing with no clean water. Over half the population are exploited by the landlords who own their slums, or else they dwell in the cardboard and jute shanty towns which are gradually encroaching on every inch of open space, even those areas of riverbank which are clearly waterlogged or unsafe.

Land-grabbers only have to fix bamboo poles in place to take possession, and the flimsy houses built on these wavering sticks are illegally rented out to families desperate to find shelter at any cost.

Then there are the once beautiful rivers Buriganga and Shitalakya. In the past they have been a lifeline for the city, providing sweet, pure water and a plentiful supply of fish, but in recent years they have become conveyors of poisonous chemicals and raw sewage. Fish no longer survive the deadly contents of these once oxygen-rich waters. Buriganga has become not only narrow, due to the indiscriminate disposal of waste and the construction of many unauthorized structures, but, even more threatening to the safety of those who live along its banks, increasingly shallow. During the annual rainy season the banks burst, leading directly to a swelling of the numbers of homeless in this urban hell-hole.

Sadly, the city is under assault from the air as well. As one of our guides pointed out, the Dhaka skyline is not blue. It's grey.

There is little sophisticated transport on the city roads and yet the vehicle population has increased ten times in the last eight years, mainly in the form of little motorized rickshaws, deadly tricycles burning the cheapest, foulest two-star petrol and spewing out the smelliest, dirtiest, blackest smoke imaginable. Being stuck in a traffic jam is a way of life in Dhaka. It may well prove a way of death. As well as lead poisoning there is the threat from carbon monoxide, which prevents blood from carrying oxygen and causes heart disease. Health experts believe the air to be so bad that it will soon become impossible to breathe.

What is so very awful about it all is that the people of Dhaka appear to accept the situation. No action is taken against the offenders. No regulations are enforced. Even the police wear masks!

Last, but sadly not in the least bit least, there is the garbage. The growing mountains of rubbish on every street corner invite disease-carrying flies and rats and produce a filthy, poisonous liquid called leachate, which contaminates the underground water. Filthy water and human excreta, poultry residue, polythene and general debris choke the drains until the rains wash them out into the rivers to provide the citizens of Dhaka with a cocktail of poisons causing diarrhoea, dysentery, jaundice and typhoid. What is more, experts have decided that much of the waterlogging problem caused by the 1998 flood was due to polythene bags clogging the already stagnant drains. From our point of view the sight of tiny market stalls selling fly-covered meat directly over open sewers and next to stinking rotten waste of all kinds was stomach-turning in the extreme.

And yet, and yet. In the midst of this noisy, frustrating, filthy city we sensed an energy, a beating pulse of determination that may overcome again one day if the cause can be made important enough to fight for.

Traffic

According to a newspaper report, in Dhaka city there are 45,600 cars, 8,600 buses, 1,500 taxis, 9,900 trucks, 1,500 auto tempos (taxis for ten passengers), 18,800 motorized rickshaws, 26,000 motorcycles, 150,000 rickshaws, 100,000 rickshaw vans and 3,000 pushcarts.

We can vouch for all this. We met every single one of them.

Rickshaws and rocking horses

A: He was just one rickshaw pedaller among many, skinny and sharp-eyed, no different from all the rest really. Those sharp eyes of his certainly glittered brightly, but only, I guessed, with the feverish desire to finish the job he was doing so that he could be paid a few taka and get on with the next one. He drove those pedals round with every ounce of strength in his thin body, the muscles on the backs of his legs standing out like two hard knots in insubstantial lengths of string. Seeing him reminded me of something. That night as I lay in bed at the guesthouse I remembered what it was.

One of my favourite short stories is 'The Rocking Horse Winner' by D.H. Lawrence. The central figure is a boy whose father has died. His widowed mother struggles to keep up appearances on a low income, but with little success. The very air is filled with financial need. The large, expensive house seems to audibly demand more money, as though it were a living thing. Desperate to help and to find release from the ever-present strain, the boy discovers that if he rides the old rocking horse in his nursery fast enough and for long enough, he is given the names of winners in horse races due to be run on the following day. With the help of the gardener and later his uncle he manages to secretly win large sums of money which are passed on to his mother without her ever guessing their origin. Unfortunately, the rocking horse has to be ridden faster and faster, and for longer and longer periods on each occasion, and still the demand for more money throbs through the house. After one last, wildly violent ride the boy calls out the name of tomorrow's winner to his uncle before collapsing with exhaustion and fever. By the end of the following day the horse has won enough money to finally solve every conceivable financial problem for the family, but the boy is dead.

That's what it reminded me of.

Apple optimists

B: There were four of them. Barefoot boys ranging in age from maybe twelve down to about six. They were setting up a cardboard box right in the thick of it, actually between the lanes of moving traffic, and at the moment I saw them, they were totally oblivious of all onlookers. Clearly not open for business quite yet, they were at the stage of carefully displaying their wares. These 'wares' consisted of about a dozen small, yellowy-coloured, battered apples which from the look of them had probably been rejected from one of the slightly more upmarket stalls operating over the open sewer on the other side of the street. This quartet of entrepreneurs were engaged with total concentration in turning these nasty little fruits so that as few bruises as possible were visible to passers-by like ourselves. After some heated debate one of them would move one of the apples through a forty-degree turn and the other three would examine the effect seriously, heads tilted, as if they were studying a masterpiece in an art gallery. Then they would either nod with satisfaction or tweak the apple a further few degrees.

I don't know what the outcome of their enterprise was, but this was perhaps my clearest glimpse of Bangladeshi optimism during the whole of our stay.

Crime in the city

On 7 Jan 12 buses were looted over a period of 12 hours but nobody came to the rescue of the affected passengers, none from the police, none from the multitudes of civilians. Late at night on Eid Day the son of a highly placed Biman official was shot dead by some of his friends. Early next morning a joint secretary to the government was the victim of muggers ... but a police control van was parked in sight of the muggers … We are faced with a situation where terrorists seem to be involved in legitimate business going about their business in full view of law and order authorities … they can pay off the police, hide behind their business' godfathers and their political mentors … We cannot deteriorate into a non-country swarming with 'godfathers' and their 'mastans', law of the strongly armed, and helplessness of democratically elected governments

Dhaka Independent, *Monday 17 January 2000*

Nothing else

B: Almost under the wheels of our car, at the very centre of the latest rickshaw jam, crouched a man. In a space no bigger than his own squatting body he had set up his stall. It consisted of a wooden orange box covered with white paper on which were displayed a few meagre bunches of bruised grapes and three small piles of oranges. As I watched, he absentmindedly peeled one of them, parting the segments with the tips of his long bony fingers and placing the result like an opened rose on to a folded square of paper. Then his eyes slid away to my right and he became motionless again, apparently unaware of the mayhem all around him. There was absolutely no attempt to engage anyone into buying his produce and I found myself wondering, 'Who, but *who*, is going to lean down from their precarious perch on a rickshaw, or open the window of their car, to purchase fruit that is lying inches away from the filthy undercarriages of this traffic?'

From the lack of expression in the unfocused eyes of the stall holder as he gazed into the distance, I guessed that he shared my pessimism. He was not expecting anyone to buy anything either, any more than anyone probably had the day before or the day before that (the fruit looked very old!)

Nevertheless, I reflected, as I sat that evening on the balcony of our guesthouse room looking down into the quiet street and pondering all we had seen that day, tomorrow he will presumably set up the same little makeshift stall with the same manky fruit, and with the same resigned lack of hope or energy. It's what he does. There's nothing else.

Street poverty

A: *Poverty comes tapping on the window of our car*
But I know the ropes
Stay quite calm, don't meet their eyes
Relationship is fatal
Register no silent questions

Offer no replies
For God's sake don't explain
Don't say
Now look, you haven't understood
I'm on your side
I'm sponsored by World Vision
An international agency
I'm here to write a book for them, here to help the poor
The profits will all go to you
Well, no, not you precisely, but to people just like you
Well, slightly younger and –
Look, just stop tapping on the window, will you?
Go away – I've told you that I care about the poor
We all do, every one of us inside this car
No, no, no, it's really not as simple as the needs you have today
You – you have to go and be where there's a project
That's the way it works – it has to be like that, you see
It's got to be well organized
These one-off payments never work, because –
Get off my window
Have you taken in a single word I've said?
It's not about your current need to eat
Try to understand
The key word is community
Social change will trickle down and help the individual to ...
Please take your hollow eyes and outstretched hand away from me
I do not want you
You are frighteningly thin
You make me feel so bad
When poverty came tapping at the window of our car
I knew the ropes

The Duke of Edinburgh syndrome

A: 'Now that,' I said earnestly to Dhiman, 'is a very interesting looking man indeed!'

This is, as we all know, the age of political correctness, and relatively naive travellers like us, being hosted in a far country, very quickly developed a tendency to shower respect, reverence and admiration indiscriminately on everything that we encountered. I suppose it was partly a reaction to the strange sense of meaningless celebrity that had been conferred on us since we landed in Dhaka. There had been much appreciative talk and apparent excitement among the very kind and helpful people we had met about the fact that we were 'famous writers from England', but as far as I could tell no one had actually read anything that we'd written. Perhaps that was just as well ...

Then there was the fact that we were white Europeans who had come to do something or other that might ultimately benefit the poor of Bangladesh. Help! We sensed in some quarters a disproportionate expectation that weighty financial or political decisions might hang on the way in which we reacted to what we were shown. In the slums themselves a white face is so unusual that crowds gathered wherever we went, particularly when we were accompanied by either a close and affectionate local family, or a little posse of World Vision workers, or a film crew, or a man with a very large and expensive camera, or all four. On one memorable occasion we stopped to buy saris at an open-fronted shop. Within minutes we found ourselves at the centre of a huge, clamouring crowd, each member of which made it his or her personal responsibility to offer opinions and advice on every single one of our choices.

Ultimately this rather bewilderingly hollow fame leaves one suffering from what I can only describe as a sort of Duke of Edinburgh syndrome. The symptoms consist of voluntarily peering like an amiable half-wit at every aspect of the environment, and enthusing with mild panic about absolutely everything for fear that one might miss or neglect something that happens to mean the whole world to somebody. I began to feel that if I heard the words Amazing! Wonderful! Tremendous! coming out of Bridget's mouth very much more I would lose my sanity and start beating her soundly with a rolled-up project report. But then, I'm just the same, so ...

Anyway, back to this very interesting man that I pointed out to our driver. First of all, I ought to say that the streets of Dhaka are by no means short of very interesting people. Some of them are simple beggars, hopeless and hungry, others are extremely artistic beggars, their individual acts (small pathetic child leading ancient blind grandfather, for instance) polished and honed to high levels of thespian professionalism. There are very upright men wearing the kind of ferocious moustaches that one associates with British military leaders of the old barking, posh school, their hair improbably cut in the severe short back and sides style that one rarely sees in England nowadays. And then there is the wide variety of holy men whose behaviour and attire were always going to baffle someone like me, who, as a paid-up member of the Church of England, finds even the behaviour and attire of Anglican clergymen slightly odd.

??????? Did you know? ???????

Every day one person in seven is very hungry.

The man I had spotted appeared to be one of these priests or holy men. Our vehicle had yet again been forced to halt by a congealed wodge of bell-ringing, horn-blasting, hooter-tooting traffic, so I was able to study him objectively for almost a minute. He was standing at the side of the road and he really did look rather impressive, a tall, intense, angular figure dressed from head to foot in some shiny black material tailored into a vaguely pantomime-like costume. He could have played Abanazar. The man's hair had been scraped to the back of his head and gathered in a sort of irregular black halo, shaped somewhat in the style of a turkey's tail-feathers. The long thin face with its fanatical eyes, its hatchet nose and its uncompromisingly narrow mouth was made impossibly longer by a thin black beard which stretched downwards for at least twenty-four inches before being carefully rolled at the end like one of those coloured paper hooter things you blow at parties. It occurred to me that the man might have done this quite deliberately in order to make a match for his long, pointed pair of shoes, the toes of which curled back on themselves in exactly the same way. Around his neck the object of my study wore a multitude of string and leather necklaces from which dangled an assortment of obscurely fashioned pendants and wooden shapes of vaguely cabalistic nature.

It was his behaviour that intrigued me most. Every now and then the tall dark figure would bend from the waist, sweeping down with one spindly arm to take up a handful of dirt or mud from the side of the road. With this he would anoint his forehead, his mouth and his chest in solemn, ceremonial manner, his lips moving rapidly as he did so. The words were impossible to hear, and I wouldn't have understood them anyway, but it appeared to me as if he must be accompanying his ritualistic actions with sacred chants or prayers.

'Dhiman,' I said, pointing, 'you see that man over there.'

He leaned across me and peered through the window.

'Aaah, yes,' he boomed in his slow, deep tones.

'Well,' I said earnestly, feeling a spot of the old D. of E. trouble coming on again, 'I'm assuming that he's some kind of priest or holy man. You see, I've noticed how he's touching himself with the very dirt from the road. It's almost as if – well, it's almost as if he's wanting to touch the essence of the city itself in – in a sort of – well, a sort of propitiatory way. I just wondered if you have a word for people like him, for people who do that kind of thing?'

Dhiman stared at the man for a few moments longer.

'Oh, yes,' he said, nodding his head wisely, 'we do have a word for men like him. We call them mad.'

'Ah ...'

Spitting

B: There is a lot of spitting on the streets of Bangladesh. A lot of extravagant throat clearing and projectile gobbing which is not, I have to say, a very attractive feature of travelling in the city. Of course it makes sense – the dust is lethal and I'm sure everyone grows up with a 'better-out-than-in' philosophy. Even so, I have to confess I am very glad our trip coincided with the Eid holiday celebrating the end of Ramadan. This important festival in the Muslim calendar makes life very hard for the whole community. For twenty-eight days no food, water or even saliva is to be swallowed from sun-up to sundown. Only the pedal rickshaw carriers, who need every ounce of their fragile strength, are exempt from this strenuous religious fast. So, through the last part of December and the first week of January all good Muslims need to be seen energetically spitting away at all times and in all places and we missed this treat by one week only! Thank you, Peter Scott. Thank you, God!

Chicken

B: Amid the Keystone Cops atmosphere of driving behind speeding rickshaws, resembling as they do those funny little early cars in old grainy films, there are patterns which recur as if we are running a single reel of film again and again. Here's that bus, its roof encrusted with bodies, there's the inevitable beggar and here's the bamboo cart with its ridiculously top-heavy load.

And, in every rerun, there's a live cockerel squawking and fluttering, its neck clutched in a fist at the end of an outstretched arm.

Why? It is almost as though some eccentric film producer has felt the need to add even more sound effects to the cacophony that already exists. After the fourth rerun I had to ask. Dhiman, our source of all wisdom, appeared surprised at my ignorance.

'They're probably on the way to visit their family for dinner. It is still the holiday period. They would never dream of arriving empty-handed.'

That I could understand. Our brief encounters with folks in this country had revealed the generosity of their natures. But it still didn't answer the crux of my question, so I tried again.

'But wouldn't it be easier to kill it first so it didn't have to flutter and squawk all over the place?' *and go through agony*, I added silently.

'But then it would not be fresh.'

End of conversation. Yet again I resigned myself to the hot flush of embarrassment that I was beginning to get used to. No cool bags, no refrigeration. Of course it made sense to transport the meat course live whenever possible.

I don't think I asked any more questions that afternoon.

Carnival

B: Everywhere in the traffic there are children. Peering out from behind their parents on countless rickshaws, perched on the front of bicycle bars, wobbling on top of sacks of flour and rice in numerous rickety bamboo carts, squatting precariously on the roofs of buses. The sheer number of children not in school on a weekday adds to the atmosphere of old-fashioned carnival. This is especially so when you pass close to them and they smile and wave, clutching the gilt support pole of their gaudy rickshaw as if they are riding something that has escaped from a carousel.

Against the tide

A: Like an Elastoplast on a severed artery, like Canute on the seashore, like a lemming who changes his mind and turns on the very edge of the cliff, so the Dhaka traffic policeman faces the multi-coloured torrent of vehicles that confronts him on each and every working day.

These brave or foolhardy men are easy enough to pick out. They wear a distinctive uniform of white, jodhpur-like trousers, blue shirts and white helmets. They are armed with a whistle (about as effective and useful as the one they give you for peeping on when you fall out of an aeroplane and land in mid-Atlantic thousands of miles away from the nearest living person), and a stick (presumably for gesturing fiercely at people). The striking and strangely plaintive thing about these uniformed men with their whistles and their sticks is that, as far as we could tell, not a single person who drove or pedalled on those wide, dusty roads took the slightest bit of notice of them.

How does one survive such a role without losing dignity?

The solution appears to lie in giving the impression that you are actually condoning and even organizing the chaos. We frequently observed one of these white-helmeted ones flattened against a pole at the side of the road, sternly waving on the oblivious, horizontal avalanche of traffic in a manner suggesting that if he were to stop his feeble hand-flapping, drivers would no longer be able to resist the hideous temptation to dawdle along in very slow, disciplined straight lines. In the same way a teacher might insist that his pupils engage in a session of informal conversation when he can't stop them chattering to each other.

I am not at all sure if, broadly speaking, this strategy is wise or foolish, the refuge of a coward or simply the strategy of a survivor, but I do know that it makes me think about the church and morality in this country at this time. Why, I wonder?

Where the heart is?

A: Okay, here's a question for you. Where would you guess that Bridget and I encountered most other white people in the course of our trip?

Restaurants? Hotels? Airports? Gift shops?

Well, for a start, I ought to tell you that the grand total of white faces in the slums and country areas amounted to – let me just add it up – yes, precisely nil, unless you counted Bridget and me, of course. Like the quantity and type of bread that my mother used to buy every day to feed three growing sons, we were two large white bloomers among myriad small brown Bangla baguettes.

Even in Dhaka, the capital, you would have to search quite long and hard before coming across a white face – unless you knew where to look, that is. So where do you think that was?

The answer, as you may well have guessed by now, was the bank. I had to go into a branch of Grindley's bank to change my sterling into taka, and there it was that I discovered a live and solemnly buzzing nest of folk with white faces, each one of them busily counting money and depositing money and withdrawing money and changing money and enquiring about money and making decisions about money, and I was one of them.

I noted my own response to being in the bank with great interest and faint dismay. One of the things we noticed very early on in our brief encounter with this chunk of the third world, is that poverty produces more irregular shapes than straight lines. In fact poverty is, in the most general terms, more attractive to look at than prosperity. Buildings and shops can be like lamplit caves or half-finished cathedrals, streets teem colourfully with lives and litter and vehicular chaos, all viewed through the ever-present veil of dust that softens sharp angles, adding a kind of filmic beauty to the scene even as it chokes your lungs.

All of this made for interesting little entries in the neat little notepads of English writers looking for material for their neat little third world book, but it also made me feel rather unsafe. I was surprised to discover the extent to which my security must have always depended upon a vague assumption that 'They' have got things more or less organized. In Great Britain streets are mended. Building regulations prevent the erection of unplanned, unsafe structures. There are rules for road-users that are actually enforced from time to time. Butchers are not allowed to display joints of meat covered in flies and hanging over open sewers. The catalogue could go on and on. Now, some may laugh as they read this list, and suggest that, in fact, such strictures are only imperfectly in place in this country, but until one experiences the sheer randomness of somewhere like Dhaka, it is impossible to understand the difference. The shapeless, unwieldy infrastructure of that dislocated city makes one feel as though its four corners are resting, as it were, on the flimsiest of flimsy stilts, and that a high wind or the addition of a little more weight could bring the whole thing tumbling down.

Rightly or wrongly, walking into that substantially built bank was like taking a draught of cold water on a boiling hot day. The tastefully decorated, high-ceilinged interior was calm, ordered, solid, civilized, full of right angles and straight lines. Conversations at the various desks and counters were being conducted in the hushed and reverential tones appropriate to the all-pervasive presence of the great god Cash, the most universally worshipped deity of all.

It is true that I certainly did experience a sense of safety for the few minutes that I spent in that cool, pristine place, but I must be honest. As I walked back out into the dusty street and the noise of traffic, I felt, fanciful though it may seem, just a little less clean than when I had walked in.

Dhiman

A: We grew very fond of Dhiman, the man who drove us throughout our fortnight in Bangladesh. A very competent and reliable individual, he was a man of few words, but one day he told us a little of his story.

Dhiman and his wife, both of the Hindu faith, very much wanted to have a child, but, for various reasons, it seemed that this was not to be. One day they attended a Christian meeting together, and were both 'zapped', or slain in the spirit, or however you like to describe the business of God deciding you are going to end up on your back when you didn't expect to. It was shortly after this experience that Dhiman's wife became pregnant. Both of them connected this happy development with events at the recent meeting, and Dhiman might have converted then and there, had it not been for his wife's fear that such a radical change of faith would arouse terribly destructive conflict in her immediate family.

'But,' said Dhiman, in his deep, deliberate tones, 'God gave my son to me, and therefore I will bring him up as a Christian.'

'And you,' we asked, after hearing this story, 'are you a Christian?'

Dhiman smiled and chuckled and would not give us a straight answer, but it didn't really matter, because after two weeks in his company we knew the answer anyway.

• TUITAL •

The road

A: Don't you just love mornings that are fresh and beautiful? That's what God served up to us early on the Tuesday when Bridget, Peter, Sujit, Dhiman and I set off for Tuital.

The road that took us away from the city was one long artificial ridge, rising like a knobbly spine above the eternal green and brown acres of rice fields, mustard plantations and occasional grazing areas for cattle and goats. Dotted around the vast plain on both sides, island villages, created to resist the inevitable floods later in the year, rose like fantastic mushrooms, crowned with foliage and jumbled buildings.

We had known that our journey from Dhaka to Tuital in the World Vision car and later by boat would be a long one. It also proved exciting, to say the least. As always, we had many reasons to be grateful that Dhiman, our super-competent driver, was in charge of the vehicle. Every now and then a bus, its passengers stuffed inside like soft toys crammed into a glass jar, or clinging to the roof and sides like barnacles, would come snorting and galloping towards us along the narrow, uneven road like an angry water-buffalo defending its territory. Each of these confrontations caused a cold weight to settle in our stomachs. We had only just read a recent article in a Dhaka newspaper about the high mortality rate in accidents involving buses on these roads. Dhiman, however, coolly played 'chicken' with the drivers of these angry monsters. He usually won, but there were times when we had to give way, swerving perilously over to the side of the road and on to the extreme edge of the ridge.

'Look,' I whispered urgently to God through my teeth after the third time this had happened, 'we want to go to heaven, but not on a beautiful morning like this.'

Nor were we free of rickshaws now that we had left the city behind. They were certainly far fewer in number, but because we were travelling at speeds that would have been impossible in the congested streets of the city, the slow-moving, manually operated vehicles constituted a much greater hazard when we met one jingling round a corner towards us or pulling out of a side road. After nine or ten of these encounters I felt as if we were inside one of the computer games my children have played over the years. The rickshaws were like those swarms of minor enemies that have to be 'eaten' or vanquished on the way to one's ultimate goal. Just as in those games, they rose up unexpectedly before us in a flash of colour, then seemed to vanish beneath our wheels as wispily and insubstantially as if they had ceased to exist at the instant when we passed them.

Every now and then our route would pass through the main street of a village, its occupants either feverishly active or totally immobile, just like their counterparts in the city. The surprisingly numerous shops were small or large, sparsely or well stocked, presumably according to the wealth of their owner, but all were uneven and amateur in construction, and all had in common the raw and asymmetrical aura of enterprises that have grown out of what is available from the land itself. Not many bank loans in this area.

'I suppose,' I said, turning to Peter as we passed through one of these villages, 'in some ways the poorest commercial bits of Victorian England must have seemed a bit like this. Lots of little caves and sheds and ramshackle buildings of all sizes lit at night by candles and oil-lamps and the occasional open fire.'

'Perhaps,' he replied, 'but I'd say it was more primitive than that – more like just before the Great Fire of London, if you ask me. Every man for himself.'

We stopped eventually to stretch our legs and drink some of the bottled water that we had brought with us. Strolling down a narrow, tree-lined track near to the place where the car was parked, I found myself indulging in a little mind game that I have played since I was a child – in fact, whenever I have found myself in alien or distant places.

Suppose, I was saying to myself, that instead of being brought here by car, I had been magically and unexpectedly transported to this place from England and had to find my way home somehow. Would I even guess that this was Bangladesh? Would I panic? What would I think when I walked up this track and found a line of those funny little shops full of people who would stop what they were doing and stare blankly at me, wondering what this strange person could be doing in their village? Would I dare to ask them for help? I supposed I would, but the whole thing felt so very alien. Shivering a little with the sense of distance and separation I turned a corner out of the trees into a large open space and then stopped abruptly. I was as good as home.

There was a game of cricket going on.

I was well aware that the Bangladeshi national team had recently achieved a famous victory over their arch-rivals, Pakistan. Now cricket fever was obviously gripping the youth of the country.

Those who have not been initiated into the universal brotherhood of cricket enthusiasts will find it next to impossible to understand why the sight of a bunch of barefoot kids playing cricket on a scrappy bit of ground at the front of a school with a cow fielding dispassionately at point brought peace to my heart. But it did. Seeing people playing cricket always has, and it always will. Those who say there will be no cricket in heaven are sadly deluded and almost certainly theologically unsound.

The remainder of our journey necessitated the crossing of two bridges, both of which featured yawning gaps right in the centre. On both of these occasions everyone except our intrepid driver bravely got out. Standing safely further along the bridge beyond the gap, we held our breath, clenched our teeth and signalled the need for minute steering adjustments with little urgent flapping movements of our hands as Dhiman allowed his vehicle to creep forward, its wheels clearing the edges of the danger zone on both sides by a matter of mere millimetres.

Full of colour, interest and alarm as it was, by the time this four-hour drive, the bumpiest of our lives, was over, we were more than ready to try some other, more gentle form of transport.

The river

B: It was one thing reading about the inferior status of women in Bangladesh, but it was quite another thing being one!

As I scrambled and slid down the muddy slope towards the river, clutching my bulging bags and hoping against hope that I wouldn't fall and make a complete idiot of myself, I reflected on this stark contrast somewhat wryly. Ahead of me, Adrian and Peter strode confidently, flanked by an army of smiling helpers who had not only relieved them of all their bags and coats but were anxiously poised ready to assist them if they slipped or needed a helping hand.

Oblivious of my plight and deep in conversation with Sujit, Adrian accepted the outstretched hand of the boatman and stepped aboard the narrow wooden vessel, which rocked violently in protest until he managed to squeeze on to the seat near the bows. By the time I got there the hand had been withdrawn and the engine kicked into action. If it hadn't been for Peter unceremoniously hauling me aboard at the last moment I think I might have ended up running along the bank.

Settling down on the narrow wooden bench under the bamboo awning I began to relax. This bit of the journey promised to be far more therapeutic than the previous four-hour rollicking ride. The sun shone from a sky of pearl and peach, and apart from emitting a perfume of petrol and sewage the river was beautiful. It was also extremely busy.

Did you ever have one of those instructive picture-books for toddlers where each page depicts a familiar scene with lots of people doing whatever the author of the book has decided that everyone ought to be doing in such a place? The picture labelled 'The Park', for instance, might include a boy flying a kite, children feeding ducks and sailing boats on the pond, babies being pushed in prams, young couples eating sandwiches on benches and park keepers picking up leaves. Well, the page that had opened before me now would have been called 'The River'. Perhaps an even better image would be of a classroom frieze gently unrolling to reveal example after example of 'Uses for the River'.

Whole families are vigorously washing their hair, their bodies, their faces and even their teeth. A few yards further on, a man and a small boy are washing down the skinny shanks of a heavily resigned ox, still harnessed to its primitive wooden plough, while, from shallower water, a woman chatters to them as she slaps and scrubs their clothes on a wooden board. A little further on, a couple of cows drink from the river, and there's a pig surrendering to the experience of being energetically scrubbed by a child who can't be more than seven years old.

As if the thought of what these animals are probably depositing beneath the tranquil surface of the water is not enough, I notice with horror simple metal pipes running directly into the river from shaky bamboo shelters. Despite this silent latrine alert, youngsters appear undeterred as they play and splash only feet away from where the pipe enters the river. Similarly unworried, a nearby group of women are collecting drinking water, cleaning their huge metal rice cooking pots, and washing their flowing brown hair.

I suppose this lack of hygiene should have had a more shocking effect, but the gentle, seemingly endless movement of our boat through drifts of emerald-coloured water hyacinths glistening on the surface of the greeny-brown water, caused the whole experience to take on a strangely Alice in Wonderland quality, in which the incongruous is perfectly normal. This dreamy feeling of fantasy was reinforced by the indisputable fact that everyone we had seen appeared to be having a very nice time indeed.

Having said all this, I made a mental note that nothing – but absolutely nothing – would persuade me to venture into the beguiling brown waters of this particular river!

I was brought firmly back to reality by hearing Adrian, reverting to Duke of Edinburgh mode, asking Sujit a question.

'What does this writing mean?'

He was pointing to two lines of elegant hand-painted script adorning the side of our boat. Having heard a great deal about the Bangladeshi people's' deep love of poetry and beautiful language I tried to anticipate the answer. Maybe the first could be a Muslim blessing. Perhaps the second was a lyrical dedication to the boat-man's mother, or the name of his beloved boat, or ...

Sujit's gravelly, friendly voice interrupted my speculations.

'The first line means, "Are you sure you haven't left anything behind?" and the second says, "Thank you, come again."'

Beside me the Duke of Edinburgh frowned and nodded. So much for poetry and speculation!

When we finally shuddered to a halt I was amused to see the pattern of priorities repeat itself, as Adrian was carefully assisted on to the bank by the welcome committee like an item of precious cargo, eager hands grabbing his bags and refusing to take no for an answer when it came to taking his coat. Watching him from behind as he ascended the slippery bank, flailing his arms to keep his balance and almost sending his beaming hosts flying in the process, I was reminded of Gulliver in Lilliput, so absurdly huge did he seem next to the Bangladeshi World Vision staff. And it was with this thought uppermost in my mind that I scrambled off the boat as unceremoniously as I had scrambled on and followed the elite up on to firm ground.

At last we had arrived in Tuital and we were going to see for ourselves whether World Vision could put its money where its mouth was, so to speak.

The priest

A: 'Would you like to come and see my little project?'

Father Parimal Rozario pointed across the kitchen garden to a little covered area where two saucer-eyed cows, their hides like softest suede, were tethered to a post, contentedly chewing wisps of hay.

'Yes, I'd love to,' I replied, following Father Parimal across the garden.

It was the third day of our stay in Tuital, and I was becoming increasingly intrigued by our host, a priest in the Roman Catholic church, and a man of many parts.

From the moment when we stepped off the boat and began to make our way up the steep mud bank towards the village and the mission house (Bridget lagging behind for some unaccountable reason), I had felt as if we were walking into the middle of one of those tales written between the wars. You know what I mean – set in some colonial outpost where the atmosphere always seems to be dripping with humidity, and the seething passion in at least one character is building up towards an explosion that is bound to neatly coincide with the beginning of the monsoon.

Not that there was much humidity in the Tuital region at this time of year, thank God. The days that we spent there were misty and invigorating in the early mornings, becoming, as Michael Fish might put it, bright and fresh by mid-morning. In Father Parimal, though, there certainly was a passion, but there was no need for it to explode because it had an outlet. The pressure of his passion for Jesus was continually expressed in deeds and words, not only towards those who would consider themselves part of his flock, but also, inspiringly, towards those who most decidedly would not.

Like many great men of God, he did not appear particularly special when we met him on that first day. A neat, smallish man with short, very black wavy hair, the top half of his body wrapped up against the 'cold' of the winter evening, he led us through locked doors into the yard of the two-storied, colonial-style mission house where he lived, and where we were to stay for three nights.

'Why does the compound have to be locked so securely?' I asked.

'Well,' he replied calmly, 'not long ago some men came here at night with guns demanding money, so ...'

When we went to bed that night Bridget and I eyed the huge iron bolts on our massively heavy, metal bedroom door with warm approval. Just the job, we thought, when it came to men with guns demanding money. Next day, though, yawning and stretching on the balcony outside our room, listening to children chuckle as they played somewhere below, savouring the dark pink of the bougainvillea on the railing in front of us and relishing the caress of the sweet, hazy morning, we found it almost impossible to believe in men with guns demanding money.

At dinner on the second day of our stay (chicken, rice and fish, of course – *how many more chicken must die so that we may live*?) the priest talked about his life and ministry in Tuital. He described to us how the priest before him had been threatened and intimidated so severely by militant, violently anti-Christian Muslims that he had been forced to live at the mission in a state of virtual siege.

'When I came here,' said Father Parimal, his even features animated by the memory, 'I made a point of walking straight into the home of the leading Muslim trouble-maker, and I said to him, "What is all this I hear about attacking Christians? Show me around, and then make me a cup of tea and tell me about it." So he showed me everything and we drank tea and became friends. He was no more trouble after that.'

He told us about the secret desire of many Muslims to become Christians, and their fear that if they did so they would have to leave home for good for fear of being killed.

'The work and generosity of World Vision,' he said, 'provides a bridge to the Muslim community which makes it much easier for me to cross over. The people have received and are grateful. I am able to tell them who they should be grateful to.'

He spoke of at least one miraculous healing that he had witnessed since coming to Tuital, and about his personal belief that Bangladesh will be a Christian country in fifty years – especially, he added, if the Blessed Virgin were to be proclaimed co-redemptress with the Lord Jesus Christ. He also expressed, among other opinions, his disapproval of birth control, other than by natural methods.

Now, here's an interesting thing – well, I think it is.

Bridget and I and Peter and Sujit sat around the long wooden dinner table that night, listening to this man expressing opinions and theology that from many points of view were completely at variance with our own, and we said not a word to contradict him. No one could have more respect for Mary, the mother of Jesus, than I have. I think she is possibly the best example of patient, quirky obedience that is available to us, but I shall never worship her or accept that her role is in any sense a redemptive one, not least because she herself would have been horrified to think that anyone could possibly see her in such a way. I believe that Jesus is the only way to salvation, and as I have already attempted to peel that onion of a statement in another book, I won't do it again here because I'll only make myself cry.

Nor did I agree with Father Parimal on such issues as birth control. If ever there was a society that needed safe and efficient birth control it must be here in Bangladesh, one of the poorest and most densely populated countries in the world.

I'm sure part of the reason for not raising any of these objections or disagreements was a general and absolutely valid feeling on our part that it would be deeply discourteous to accept a man's hospitality with one hand and offer the opinion that he was seriously in error with the other, but it wasn't just that. It wasn't even mainly that.

Of course I can only speak for myself. For me it was something to do with the fact that, when I had asked this man how he felt about Jesus, his face became illuminated by one of those smiles that are born only out of contact with God. It was something to do with the fact that he was patently loved and respected by adults and children alike, as we had clearly seen when we walked beside him among the local people. And, most important of all perhaps, it was to do with him simply being here in this place, solidly committed to a dangerous and challenging situation, doing the job that God had given him to do. He seemed to be doing it, moreover, in an unusually Jesus-like way, the voice of his reaching-out echoing that intriguing combination of bold holiness and shockingly ordinary humility that made and makes Jesus so very attractive and so very infuriating, depending on who and where you happen to be when you encounter him. In other words, in the context of obediently fulfilling the call of God on my life, in the place where I am supposed to be, I am not sure that I am not more in error than Father Parimal Rozario. I think I shall leave God to work out the theology.

'What exactly is your project?' I patted one of the cows on the side of its neck, and the handsome creature raised its huge, Bambi-like eyes solemnly towards mine for a moment before returning to the hay.

'I want to use my cows as a teaching aid so that the people will see all the benefits that can come from keeping cattle. I will teach them about feeding and milking and raising calves and all the other things they need to know.'

'And are two cows enough?'

He leaned over to scratch between the horns of the nearest animal as he replied. The cow bobbed its head gently but seriously in appreciation.

'I have two. I have written to the prime minister to ask him to give me a third, and he has said he will. Really, it would be good if I had a fourth cow. That would be just right – perfect.'

'How much is a cow?'

'Well, a quite good cow is ten thousand taka, but the best sort of cow, the sort I would really like to have – an Australian cow, that would be twenty thousand taka.'

It didn't take much working out. Slightly less than one hundred taka to the pound, so the good Australian cow would cost somewhere around two hundred pounds. It seemed to me, as I stood beside the priest in the warm winter sunshine, that there was something very solid and real and achievable about a cow, something that really could be done.

'We'll buy you one,' I said. 'Our church at home will buy you one. We'll club together and buy you a fourth cow. I know people will want to do that.'

And I was right. They do want to do that, and that's exactly what we're going to do. There's something about a cow ...

The question

A: Anyone who had been walking behind Sujit and me as we strolled from Father Parimal's compound towards the first village we were due to visit in Tuital, would have been able to observe a neat little visual aid illustrating Christian unity. I am exceptionally tall and Sujit is exceptionally short. We two Christian brothers must have looked like a stick of overweight celery promenading with a radish.

Sujit was wonderful. He had been a freedom fighter in the war for independence, and yet was one of the gentlest and most attractive personalities we have ever come across. His warmly engaging way of communicating with all people, and especially children, was a pleasure to behold.

As we walked it struck me yet again that, in a way, Bridget and I had cheated by coming to Bangladesh in January. The air was so very soft, the sun so warm and gentle on our faces, the environment so peaceful and attractive, the view across the plain such a shimmeringly blue-green, watercolour dream that it really did feel as if we had happened upon a little corner of Paradise. Countless numbers of those little island villages, the 'mushrooms' we had seen from the car, rose from the dead flat land, their stalks eaten into by the ravenous waters of past floods. Sujit explained that they were populated by folk who, Noah-like, keep boats in a dry land because they know, by bitter experience rather than prophecy, that the deluge will certainly come. These semi-accidental sculptures, created by puny, optimistic mankind under pressure from the huge forces of nature, affected one part of my mind strangely, awaking half-forgotten childhood dreams of cosily manageable, happily limited little worlds, painted in storybook colours.

When the floods came it would be hell, but I would only see that on the television.

The occasional child or group of children, wide-eyed at the sight of our white faces, passed us on the path as it wound around the fields. Sometimes a man on a bicycle would pedal carefully by. Rice shoots were being painstakingly planted out. There was a boy tending a herd of pigs. The glowing bowl of the sky was unbelievably vast. Disaster seemed a million miles away. A good moment perhaps to ask Sujit a question that I had been saving up for some time.

'Sujit,' I said, 'you really love your country, don't you?'

He chuckled deep in his throat before answering.

'Yes, yes, I love it!'

'What do you love most about it?'

'Mm.'

Clearing his throat, he stared at the ground and thought for a moment.

'Adrian, it is the green,' he said, lifting his head and indicating the landscape around us with a sweep of the arm, and again, more softly, 'I love the green of my country. Most of all, though, I love the simple, honest folk in the rural areas. One day,' he added confidingly, 'I plan to go back to my own village in the north of the country and live there and be a minister to the people there.'

'I see.'

And that was the long and the short of it.

The group

B: There must have been about forty of them, gloriously clothed in saris made in every brilliant colour combination imaginable, chattering like exotic birds as they sat closely packed together on the dirt floor in the centre of their village. Ranged all around were their menfolk and children, but this morning it was the women who were the stars. Only when you place this in the context of the low importance women are usually given does the significance of this group really come into focus. For these women have become the key to the future prosperity of their community. They are the village savings group, and their dedicated efforts have enabled them to present their husbands with the means to survive at least some of the evils that this volatile climate is always likely to throw at them.

The way it works is this. First the women attend an adult literacy class run by a World Vision volunteer. Here they learn to write their names and do very simple sums in order to be able to open an account at the bank. Then a facilitator is chosen and trained more fully and a savings group is formed. Each member must commit herself to saving what little she can afford every month. For some it may be more than others but it must be a minimum of twenty taka (20p) a month. Then, once they have saved a reasonable amount between them, they can approach World Vision for a low-interest loan for one or two individuals who have been chosen after group discussion, and who have committed themselves to paying back the loan. Government credit programmes and traditional banks are not interested in offering affordable loans to the poor. They are viewed as high risk and as yielding low returns. Even if these impoverished people do manage to secure a loan, interest is so high that they can never repay the loan and are consequently held even more securely in the poverty trap.

World Vision, in common with other aid agencies, holds a totally different view. Quoting directly from their own literature:

When you give somebody something you're saying: 'Here you are, poor person,' and the poor person is saying, 'Thank you, thank you.' But in the case of a loan, you're on the same level. You say, 'Here is a resource that you can use. Pay me back later.' And the poor person says, 'Okay, I'll be responsible for paying this back.' With work a good return can be made. When people feel that what they have achieved has been through their own efforts, it changes their lives.

As the loan will only be up to two and a half times what they have saved we are talking about investment in small but essential projects, such as buying livestock which can be used not only to feed the

???????? Did you know? ?????????

The world spends:

$780 billion on the military,
$435 billion on advertising,
$400 billion on illegal drugs and
$12 billion on perfumes?

The United Nations Food and Agricultural Organization reckons it would cost:

$8 billion to help the world feed itself and
$9 billion to provide clean water.

The World Bank believes an increase of $10 billion would lift 25 million people out of poverty.

Taken from World Vision *magazine, issue 22*

family but also to generate a little income. Considerable group pressure on those who have borrowed to repay ensures the success of the scheme. Over the years, thousands of small loans have been made and paid back throughout the Third World.

This morning, though, belonged to this little group in Tuital and they knew it.

Peeping from under the cowls of their head covering they shyly answered Adrian's questions as to how much they had saved and how they had spent their loans. Together they had saved a staggering three thousand pounds. One woman had used her loan for an irrigation pipe to water her husband's paddy field. Another had bought manure to grow vegetables. Another, potatoes. Another, a boat. Another, a goat. One modestly mentioned a cow. One woman had taken advantage of the fact that as soon as she had repaid her first loan she was eligible for another to buy a house for her family.

'How does it make you feel to be able to help your husband and your family in this way?' I asked.

Nothing so far in our encounter with these unassuming, modest women had prepared us for the explosion of sound which greeted my question. Throwing decorum to the winds they all talked at once, eyes dancing with pride, laughing and nodding.

'GOOD,' our translator told us unnecessarily,' they feel GOOD!'

Suddenly I wanted to cry, and to cover my emotion I applauded them loudly. To my joy they joined in, clapping, chattering and smiling at each other. Then the menfolk and the children joined in.

I might even have heard a few angels as well, although I can't be sure.

What I can be sure of is that World Vision and other aid agencies who follow similar practices have discovered a way of empowering these undervalued women that can only be described as Jesus-like. Over the fortnight we were in Bangladesh we met several similar groups and heard of many different uses to which they had put their loaned money. A caesarean, an operation for a child, education, sewing machines, latrines, rickshaws and even shops were just some of the answers we received from the various groups from villages and slums, but one thing they all had in common. Whenever I asked the question,

'And how does it make you feel?' we received the same ebullient response:

'GOOD! It makes us feel GOOD!'

The love

A: I have already said that one of my main concerns about going to Bangladesh was a fear that, as a result of our trip, I might ultimately feel disappointed with the work of World Vision. After all, I wasn't employed by them, and, broadly speaking, I knew nothing about the organization. They might turn out to be a useless, inefficient bunch of theoretical do-gooders who brought nothing but confusion and unhappiness into the lives of those they were supposed to be trying to help. The whole exercise could have been a disaster, a great deal of money might have been wasted, and this book would probably never have been written.

Well, it might have been like that, but if you have already read as far as this you will know perfectly well that I had no need to worry. The undeniably beneficial effects of the immense variety of work done by World Vision was a revelation and a personal inspiration to both of us. And thank God for that!

If you asked me to choose one moment or experience that exemplifies these very positive memories, I would have to select a brief statement from one of the ladies in the village savings group that Bridget has described. This wonderfully colourful collection of people had described the way in which their group works, and told us about some of the specific things that had been bought or paid for as a result. It was all very impressive.

'But tell me,' I asked, 'why do you think these workers come and help you to set up schemes like these? Why do they do that?'

There was a short pause, then one of the ladies nearest to me spoke quickly, her few words triggering many of the others into enthusiastic agreement.

I turned enquiringly to Brownson, our translator and the leader of the project. He obliged us with just four words of translation, and I reckon that the newest and humblest employee in the smallest corner of the least statusful department of the World Vision offices in Milton Keynes should read those four golden words with pleasure and pride.

'World Vision loves us.'

The written word and the race for home

B: As we finally took our leave of this delightful community I felt excited – so many facts and feelings.

Hearing from members of the community about times during the floods of 1998 when World Vision had literally saved thousands of lives by bringing in boats, food, water and blankets to families who were able to stay at home, and rescuing hundreds clinging to existence on the roofs of their collapsing dwellings, had filled me with pride in simply being associated with them.

Taking Christmas cake (a sweet pastry turnover stuffed with a coconut filling) and tea, albeit tea loaded with sugar, in the home of one of the savings group members, I had felt equally privileged. I was full of admiration for what these women had managed to achieve through sheer determination and hard work.

I had been enchanted by the children we met, especially Laurence, a little sponsor boy who, when he saw us approaching along the narrow winding track between the mustard fields, had exploded joyfully out of the doorway of his bamboo house and come hurtling down the slope to stand beaming proudly, chest puffed out like a little pigeon, ready to be introduced to the special visitors identifiable by the garlands of paper flowers round their necks. (Adrian looked very cute in his!)

Above all, though, I had been moved beyond measure by Sima Rane. Aged eleven, she had been sponsored since she was seven, and she had that air of being 'specialled' that I was coming to associate with the families of sponsor children. Her long, freshly washed hair fell in neat, thick plaits around her oval dark face, and her eyes shone with intelligence. She was wearing what was clearly her very best dress. It was lovely. Made from deep pink cotton printed with small white daisies, it was both delicate and modest, and so very feminine.

Not for the first time I thought a little ruefully of my perpetually jeans-clad daughter and her friends who, at eleven, had despised dresses as something they would not wear at any cost.

Needing to be able to remind myself what she was called, I asked her if she could write her name in my notebook, a request which seemed to galvanize the female members of her family. They crowded around her in a veritable frenzy of interest. They had loved having their photographs taken and had been intrigued by the idea that they might appear in a book, but this simple request seemed to symbolize something much more important. It proved to be the first indication of many, that education for little girls was a golden egg to be coveted and prized above all else, the gateway to a freedom and dignity unthinkable in their generation. Breathing over her shoulders, tongues between teeth, the women watched intently as Sima Rane Talukdere carefully formed each letter of her name. The audible sigh of relief as she lifted her pen from the paper was followed by a shaking of heads in sheer wonderment at the brilliance of their little celebrity.

As I waved and shook hands and salaamed for the last time and we set off on foot for the next stage of our tour of the Tuital projects, my thoughts were naturally anticipating with interest what we might encounter next. Walking companionably with a now slightly more confident member of the team, I was brought abruptly out of my reverie when I became aware that the forward posse of Adrian and his cohorts had come to an abrupt halt. There was an animated discussion going on, and a decision had just been arrived at by the time I joined them. I gathered that Adrian wished to go no further, but wanted to return to the compound immediately. Puzzled, but politely reverent, Brownson had agreed that the day's' visiting was at an end. The news, as passed to my escort, appeared to be that the great writer needed to return to start writing his important book.

Curiouser and curiouser.

There was a faint desperation in Adrian's eyes that didn't seem to quite fit the facts as given, but there was no doubting the determination with which he turned to head for home. His pace seemed to be quickening and, to my considerable amusement, soon the whole group was first lengthening its stride, then leaping, running and practically galloping to keep up with their leader as he strode more and more forcibly towards the compound. What was going on?

Presumably they thought the muse was upon him, but by now I wasn't at all convinced by my husband's motivation and was beginning to get an inkling of what was going on.

As we charged into the outer courtyard and Adrian headed for the stairs without even a word to his puffing fellow travellers I knew why we had abandoned the afternoon's programme. Muse my foot. The lunchtime curry had done its worst and Adrian was heading for, yes, you've guessed, the toilet.

Toilets in general and this one in particular

A: While we're on the subject of toilets – many years ago a friend of mine and I rather foolishly went into a wood near his home in Wadhurst (at night, would you believe!) to do a spot of birch-jumping. Yes, 'loony' is the word you're groping for.

We had been inspired by Robert Frost, a fine American writer, who describes this activity in one of his poems. It consists of climbing to the top of a slender birch tree, then releasing your legs and holding on tightly with your hands so that, in theory, you sink gently to the ground as your weight causes the tree to bend. This may have been all very romantic for Robert Frost, he obviously knew how to pick the right tree. My friend did not. His tree folded its arms and refused to bow down. The subsequent fall from a great height resulted in a severely injured back and a lengthy stay in hospital. There, being immobile and horizontal, my friend was forced to use a bedpan. So frustrated did he become by this daily indignity that he asked his wife to bring in brightly coloured leaflets advertising various types of pedestal toilet. These he stuck to the walls around his bed, gazing lustfully at this little gallery of naked porcelain

??????? Did you know? ?????????

Flushing the toilet once uses fifty litres of water. This is the amount one person needs for a survival level of drinking water, adequate sanitation, food sanitation and food preparation.

beauty in between bedpan sessions as though it was some form of pornography.

There were times during our stay in Bangladesh when I remembered my friend and his pamphlets. The toilet in our apartment at Far Pavilions was – praise God! – an entirely familiar, western model, but some of the others were not. Instead of a bowl and a seat on which you sat, there were two ceramic pads on which you placed your feet so that you could squat on your haunches.

Yes, it is worth dwelling on for a moment – the thought, I mean.

How the less athletic members of the community manage in those particular circumstances is beyond me.

It is also worth mentioning, in passing, the toilet in the corner of our bathroom at Tuital, the one I was so anxious to return to. This was certainly a conventional lavatory bowl with a flush system, but it reminded me of those stories you read in Greek mythology about a fiend who lies sleeping, only to awake with thunderous cries of wrath when disturbed by a mere mortal. The non-regulated flush system on this thing was nothing short of explosive. Following sounds like the Forth Bridge collapsing into a breaker's yard a veritable cataract of water erupted with a mighty roar from somewhere inside the bowl, filling it immediately and overflowing on to the bathroom floor in less than two seconds if the handle was not immediately returned to its original position. After only one heart-stopping experience of this phenomenon my instinct became to grit my teeth, push the handle one way, instantly push it back again, then run for dear life. That toilet scared me.

I am, by the way, deeply indebted to Bridget for so graphically describing my race for home at Tuital, when even the thought of this roaring monster seemed, for that very stiff-legged, short period, sweeter than life itself.

Of course, even the squatting-on-your-haunches model was the height of civilization compared with what is available to the vast majority of Bangladeshi folk on the streets and in the slums. Here, unless a project has installed slab latrines, the open sewer at the side of the road and the corner of a field behind a block of dwellings tend to be the only options.

If Graham Kendrick hasn't yet written a chorus of praise and thanksgiving for pedestal flush toilets it's jolly well time he did. We won't have to do actions with it, though, will we?

• WEEKEND ALARMS AND EXCURSIONS •

Fever

A: All my darkest and most dreadful nightmares about being ill in a country far from home seemed to be coming true towards the end of our first week away.

It began early on the Thursday afternoon of that first week, the day when we returned from Tuital, with the sudden, stomach-lurching realization that I was supposed to be writing and sending two articles to two different publications by tomorrow at the latest. Two! One would have been awful but just about feasible. Two! Being made as I am, my first response was to wilt like an unwatered lupin (an analogy drawn from bitter experience). The fact is that both Bridget and I were already wrestling with a shadowy fear that this whole bizarre Bangladesh exercise was some kind of cosmic test or exam that we were very unlikely to pass, even if they let us mark our own papers so that we could cheat. Why do I, in particular, always default to an assumption of failure? Much of my most vigorous activity is akin to that of a lazy child who rushes around feverishly cleaning up just before his parents return. I suppose that helps to explain my second response.

What could I do to make everything all right so that everyone in the world would still love me? Wandering out on to the balcony I gazed across the jumbled tops of houses towards the centre of the city, looking for inspiration. Something caught my eye. For one passing, puzzling moment I thought I was looking at a British-style cathedral in the far distance. I wasn't, of course. It turned out to be yet another building under construction, festooned with sacking, bristling with bamboo poles, the whole thing magically transfigured by a hazy shroud of smog. I sighed as I considered my lifelong love affair with cathedrals.

An idea struck me. One of those blessed articles was for a newspaper in Holland, the other for an English periodical. Dutch people were unlikely to read the English magazine, and only the Dutch ever actually learn Dutch, a language that requires its users to speak as if their mouths are full of Lego. Why should I not send the same piece of writing to both publications? Yes! Yes, I could do that!

Having borrowed a laptop computer, I sat down at the small table in our hotel room to write a deeply considered, multicultural masterpiece on my first impressions of Bangladesh. I may well be wrong, for my personal history offers a multitude of similar occasions to select from, but I cannot recall ever feeling less like writing a thousand words than I did on that Thursday afternoon. Wise words from the book of the prophet Nike, son of Adidas, sustained me. 'Just do it.' Only my pride and my fingers were willing, though. The other parts of me clenched themselves and each other miserably, waiting for the job to be over and done with.

As I saved my work and leaned the top of my body wearily over the back of the chair, my head was spinning and I seemed to be in the grip of a slight fever.

Later, we set off along the noisy, darkening streets to find somewhere to eat with our new friend and guide, Sanjay Sojwal. Sanjay is World Vision's senior communications officer for the whole of Asia, and he had come to take photographs, supervise the film crew that would be arriving on Monday, and to take over from Peter, who was due to fly back to the UK that evening.

By now I was feeling quite ill and rather worried. Suppose, I thought, I were to become really poorly for any length of time, what would become of our trip and its purpose? What on earth was God up to?

Sanjay turned out to be a highly intelligent and quite delightful companion, but it is impossible to escape the conclusion that, on that first evening, I must have presented to him as nothing more than a dull-witted Coca-Cola addict. For some obscure reason I ordered *two* bottles as soon as we took our seats, and then sat vacantly with my hand curled round one of them, finding a pathetic crumb of comfort in the coolly familiar, universal shape of the slim-waisted bottle. I ordered fish – grilled red mullet I think it was – but as soon as it arrived I wished from the bottom of my stomach that I hadn't. That red mullet may have been dead, but its spirit lived on. It was a large, fleshy fish, lying heavily on its side so that one huge, perfectly round eye was able to stare reproachfully up at me.

'There was a time,' quoth the eye dolefully, 'when I too believed that life had a meaning and a purpose, but now – well, as you can see, that time has passed. Tell me, what are *you* doing in Bangladesh?'

Hypnotized by the eye, I shook my head silently from side to side. I didn't know. I had no idea. Wiping my bedewed forehead with the back of one hand, and feeling a vague obligation to eat the dish that had been set before me, I used the other hand to poke the side of my fish with a fork. The eye seemed to widen to the size of a dartboard. I laid my cutlery down, knowing that there would be no point in picking it up again that evening. Suddenly I felt very sick and horribly dizzy and I desperately wanted to go home.

Illness that forces me to stay in bed does usually have one or two very positive aspects. It is the only time when I am able to abandon the fulfilment of my responsibilities, or perhaps more honestly, it's the only time when I'm able to abandon the drip-fed guilt caused by *not* fulfilling my responsibilities. Such a relief! It wasn't like that this time, though. Bridget and I had put an immense amount of emotional and organizational effort into our trip. Then there were World Vision workers in Great Britain as well as Bangladesh. They had gone to enormous lengths to make the project a success, however hazy the exact nature of that success might seem to us at the moment.

I lay awake for hours on that eternal Thursday night, streaming with perspiration, aching in every joint, my mind pumping out dismal images of the following day, when Bridget and I were scheduled to meet our sponsor child for the first time. We'd worried about false emotion. Huh! What a marvellously cosy luxury of a problem that was beginning to appear. Bridget would have to do it on her own now, and if this blasted illness persisted it was possible that I might never meet Shahnaj. Never meet her! What a nonsense that would make of the stupid book we were supposed to write when we got back. *If* we got back. *If* I survived. Really, when you thought about it, what was the point of it all? What was the point of anything, come to that? Nothing but randomness and falling kites and endlessly repeated negative patterns and dentists and disappointment and death playing the final hand ...

Thus, raving and raging and sweating I crossed my particular desert towards the dawn, eventually collapsing into the centre of an inadequate but welcome little oasis of exhausted, uneasy sleep.

Poets

B: This morning, having slept very little, I wake with a splitting headache and a feeling of doom. Immediately I remember what it is. Today Adrian is due to lead a writers' workshop, but will he be able to? I somehow get him propped up in bed and will him to be better.

'Would you like to try getting out of bed just to see if maybe you feel a little better?' I say gently, but, I confess, with determined hopefulness.

Adrian pulls himself out of bed, stands up, sways and sits down heavily.

'I'm really sorry, Bridget,' he says in a rather unsteady voice, 'but I do feel horribly dizzy. I'm afraid I just can't do it.'

Even I have to admit in my heart that it would be difficult to facilitate a writers' workshop from a horizontal position, and that is the only position he is going to be able to adopt safely.

'I feel so dreadful,' he goes on, 'I know how important this is to Martin and now it's too late for him to let them know.'

It is indeed. I leave my sad specimen of manhood shivering dismally in bed and go into the other room where Adrian's briefcase bulges with all the trip information. I fish out the letter from Martin Adhikary, who bears the grand title of National Church Relations Co-ordinator, and, sitting on the plumpy red sofa, try to decide what to do.

Martin happens to be one of the most delightful people I have ever met, enthusiastic, warm and extremely energetic. He is also very committed to his job, and has already told us how much he was hoping to encourage young Bangladeshi writers in this workshop. The letter before me is addressed to 'Respectable Christian Writers in Bangladesh' and invites them to meet 'our distinguished visitor' Mr Adrian Plass (a writer of great repute in Britain!!) who is to speak on 'the primary role and responsibilities of a Christian writer in a developing society in the new millenium'.

'Oh, no, he isn't,' I murmur to myself, 'I am. The respectable writers of Bangladesh are going to be addressed a) by a woman and b) by someone who has had one book published and is not in any shape or form a distinguished visitor. Poor Martin, poor writers.'

I deliberately block out any thoughts of having to cope with meeting Shahnaj on my own in the afternoon and go to have breakfast. At least, I discover myself thinking grimly, they can't serve me last today! My mood is not improved by the fact that I have been a mosquito banquet throughout the night and my face is covered in itchy red bumps.

Half way through my omelette I pull myself together. I haven't had to get up at six in the morning to share a latrine with countless others or join a queue to pump water to wash from a well several blocks from where I live. I haven't had to provide some sort of meal for six people living in a house smaller than our garden shed. I am not feeling sick or shivery like Adrian. And fortunately I do have a folder full of Adrian's stuff that I can read. Maybe if I just stick to reading stuff it will be okay. Then, surely, it will just be a case of suggesting a topic on which they can write, and all will be well. After all, they are described as young and inexperienced so they probably haven't ever attended a writing workshop before, so ...

They turn out to be not all young, and they certainly are not inexperienced. As they stand one by one to introduce themselves I am quite overcome by how accomplished and experienced they are as writers, except for one who confesses to never having written anything at all and only being there to accompany his daughter who has.

'Ah yes,' comes a loud voice from across the room, 'but he was a freedom fighter.'

Cheers and applause follow this and I reflect yet again on the fact that in this young and passionate country those who fought for its independence are heroes of every situation they find themselves in, even a seminar for writers.

Now it is my turn, and apologizing profusely for Adrian's absence I begin to describe the origins of his writing career and the link between his breakdown and consequent passion for communicating the love of God. It is into an atmosphere of sympathy and interest that I try to explain how Adrian has discovered that universal and deep truths can be communicated through simple family incidents. I share some of what we call the Katy stories, times when our daughter, especially when she was a little girl, said or did something which Adrian has been able to use to reflect our foolishness and God's love for his children. This seems to interest most of them, if nods and smiles are any indication, and it is with growing confidence that I turn to his poems. After all, I had been told there is a long tradition of poetry writing in Bangladesh, their most famous poet Tagore being held in high regard.

As I come to the end of one of my favourites, I sense something is not right. A dullness has crept into the atmosphere. They look disappointed. I choose another and this time, probably through desperation, I inject rather more passion into the reading than would be considered normal. They lean forward. At the end there is a murmur of appreciation. I begin again and this time give my rendition of 'A Winter Waking' even more welly. Now I have them, and as I finish the last line, conscious that I am beginning to sound more like Edith Evans than Bridget Plass, there is a round of applause. Now it is their turn and as I set them the task of using an illustration from something closely familiar to life in Bangladesh to communicate a truth far more universal in application, I am relieved to see pens and notebooks in use. Having said that, there is also a good deal of loud conversation and I feel rather like an inadequate prefect in charge of detention! At last their time is up and I sit back, relieved that my part is over and Martin is now in charge.

'Now before we read what we have written,' says Martin smiling, 'are there any questions?'

Having fielded a fierce, 'Why are we sitting in a beautiful room reading poetry while our people starve?' and attempted a concise response to 'What is the difference between the Christian writer and the non-Christian writer?', Martin agrees that it is fine if they want to read in Bangla and sits down.

As I listen to almost everyone reading in their own language I realize why they were disappointed by my earlier, tame readings, and why they only responded enthusiastically when I began to intone like Henry Irving. Bangla is a tonal language, its rising and falling inflections giving meaning and definition to each word. It is velvety and musical with none of the hard edges of western European languages. One by one the writers rise to their feet and declaim their work with passionate intensity. It is all very, very moving. The only problem is that not only do I not have a clue what they were talking about, but also I don't know whether what they have written is good, bad or utter rubbish! This doesn't matter, except that at the end of each one there is a long pause, with yet another bright-faced, expectant poet looking directly at me for a response.

The situation is not entirely helped by Martin occasionally leaning over and whispering rather loudly, 'That one was very good.'

I smile and mumble and clap like a clockwork clown until the last writer has finished, but then comes one more question.

'In Bangladesh we Christian writers suffer for what we write. We use our poetry to pierce the armour of unjust government and Muslim domination. Why does Adrian not use his wit to attack your government's liberal attitudes to the growing power of the Muslim community in Britain?'

Just for one moment I feel really, really fed up with my husband for having the audacity to get ill, but then it is as if I sense that my reply matters to God. I try to lean back and hear what he would like me to say.

'In our country we find that if you attack too directly it can have the opposite effect to that which you want. People simply say 'I don't have to read this rubbish' and they don't. What Adrian tries to do is to make people laugh and relax, then, while the critical side of their brain is not looking, slip in under the eye of their guard and attack the heart.'

It sounds rather good actually, and I see my husband's reputation growing before my very eyes. A sort of literary freedom fighter! I hope I haven't overdone it, aware that if I carry on like this I'll be in danger of creating a saint. I hurry on.

'The thing is, Adrian has been given the job of digging the ground ready for God to plant his seeds. For example, many men in our country don't feel the need to believe in God, so Adrian wrote this to try to stir them up. I read, 'When I Became a Christian' in my new dramatic style, only stumbling when I come to the line 'A quick salvation sandwich and a cup of sanctity' – they'll never get that – and sit down utterly exhausted, but relieved that I have managed to get through my ordeal.

The moderator rises to his feet and, after thanking everyone for coming, explains that all are welcome to stay for cakes and – turning to me with a twinkle – a cup of sancti-tea!

Showered with the published works of the entire group and promising photocopies of all the poems I have read out, I remind myself of Adrian's favourite adage, 'All gigs pass', and try to prepare my mind for the afternoon visit to Hazaribagh slum.

The slums

The squalid conditions prevailing in the slums where more and more people from rural areas are taking shelter should be a matter of great concern to urban development planners. The planners must be aware of the fact that most of the slums pose a serious health hazard. They should take note of the ever worsening crime situation which has a lot to do with the slums and the ever growing ranks of unemployed youths. The task is not easy as the rural poor, pauperized by natural calamities and the absence of employment opportunities move to the urban areas in the hope of a better life. The vulnerability of these people is fully exploited by the urban touts and muscle men and many of them end up in the world of crime.

Dhaka Independent, *Monday 17 January 2000*

My gift

B: The veil is about to be lifted.

We have driven through oldest Dhaka until the noisy, tacky glamour of the painted rickshaws and optimistic street traders has given way to increasingly narrow streets with tiny dirty shops, where flies, filth and open sewers create the rotting stench of decay. At last we bump to a halt in a small square outside what I am informed is the community centre, where Shahnaj and her friends will be waiting for me. The door opens and as we step into the dark interior, Joanna Rossario, who is in charge of the project, speaks.

'Do you recognize her?'

Everyone is smiling and I send up a prayer of prayers. 'Please let me recognize her from her last photo. Please, Lord, don't let me let her down.'

There is no need whatsoever for me to worry. Standing in front of me is a group of children, clearly dressed up in their very best clothes. They are all beaming but only one of them has a lightbulb lit up inside her. Only one shines with a confidence I have rarely seen in any child. Her hair done up in delightful rag bunches, she dazzles me with her smile and then, just as I struggle with exactly how to greet this child who doesn't know me but who is joined in such a strange way to me and my family, she steps forward and proudly gives me a full-blown red rose. Then, with a gesture which instantly establishes that as far as she is concerned I am her possession, she takes my hand. I reach into my bag and awkwardly, one-handedly produce one of my small wrapped gifts, a set of hairbrushes. I give it to her expecting her to open it, worried that it might not be suitable. To my surprise, after thanking me she hands it unopened to the slightly older girl standing next to her. There is a pause. Some conversation takes place between Shahnaj and Joanna. I stand, smile fixed in place, feeling extremely large and rather foolish and wishing Adrian was with me.

There is a sudden flurry of activity. We are to go to her home. Right now. She is ready. She knows what to do. Steering me like some kind of farm animal on the end of a rope, she hauls me forward, pointing out the safest places to put my feet to avoid falling into the sewer, gesturing upwards to where the edges of rusty corrugated iron roofs threaten to slice open my head, dismissing with shrill authority those who gather in front of us, but who, in her opinion, have no part in her celebration, ordering a small boy who turns out to be her brother to run ahead, presumably to tell her mother we are on our way. And all the time she chatters. Lifting her face to mine with total joy she chatters without ceasing, clearly unaware that I can understand not one word of what she is saying. I become aware of the other, older girl hurrying along with us. It is Shahnaj's sister, carrying my unwrapped present. Shyly she takes my other hand and, gaining confidence almost immediately, joins in the chattering. I am completely entranced, if a little breathless. I begin to feel if we go much faster down these ever-narrowing alleyways we'll start to fly! Now we are so far ahead of the rest of the party that I can reasonably suggest we stop and wait, and I am amused to see the slight anxiety on the faces of the pursuing group as they round the corner and see that I have not been abducted by my small enthusiastic charges.

We make the last part of the journey in single file as the makeshift walls are now less than three feet apart. Dark, open doorways reveal glimpses of women and children but I can see nothing very clearly, determined as I am not to disgrace myself by arriving for tea with a foot covered in sewage! We have arrived. There are two steps leading to the doorway and I make a mental note of the fact that the house appears to be built on stilts. With Shahnaj in front and her sister behind I feel we are like the carriages of a toy train shunting into the station. It is dark and it is very, very small and seemingly full of shining white teeth. Standing in front of me is a tall thin man who shyly shakes my hand.

Almost the whole area is taken up with a double bed on which are perched two grinning boys, one the lad I've already met and the other an older teenager. Shahnaj and her sister, Simon, immediately scramble up on to the bed and urge me to join them, which I do. This is just as well, because by the time Sujit, Joanna and Peter join us there is about five inches spare standing space! A commotion at the door heralds the arrival of the woman of the house, her face alight, a baby in her arms. Now there are no inches at all and as a crowd of children have blocked the doorway it all bears a marked resemblance to what one imagines must have been the conditions in Noah's ark.

There is another grinning pause as everyone waits for me to do something. But what? I reach for my bag and hand out my gifts. Oh dear, I haven't really brought the right things at all. Whatever will Shahnaj's dad and older brother make of their box of Ferrero Rochers? Will her little brother, who seems to be about eight, be very disappointed with his notebook and pencils? Why, oh why didn't I check the ages of the family before coming? I give Simon and her mother selections of soaps and toiletries and thank God that I have brought brightly coloured books, one of which I give the baby 'for when she's older', and one to Shahnaj with a T-shirt we'd bought at Heathrow. I wait for them to open their presents or to show a response, but something is wrong. The smiles have faded. What have I done? An uncomfortable silence has fallen. Oh, my goodness – what have I done? Have I broken some law of protocol? Inadvertently insulted someone in the family? Then Shahnaj whispers to her mother, who holds up both her hands in a gesture of despair and says something to Joanna, who turns to me.

'They are very sad,' she says, 'because they have no gift for you.'

Somehow God gives me the right words. 'Seeing Shahnaj is my gift.' The smiles are back, breaking up the darkness like jewels in a cave. Now everyone is talking. They have forgotten all their questions. It is enough that I am here. They have waited so long. How many children have I? Four? My word, what happiness that seems to give them! The baby is pushed into my arms. I hope against hope that I can show how able I am as a mother. God obviously doesn't feel I deserve any more divine assistance. The baby howls! I hand her back ruefully to Shahnaj's mother. Snuffling and rubbing her dark eyes with a chubby hand the baby falls asleep. We smile at each other. No translation needed. I feel a newly familiar, skinny little hand creep into mine. Shahnaj shares our moment, putting her finger to her lips.

Suddenly it's time. Time to go. Right now. Another sudden decision is made with the jerkiness that I am getting used to. Now there is a ludicrous tangle of people occupying the three square feet of standing room. Much talking. Much reassurance that it is not a sad moment because we will be back on Sunday and Adrian will be with us (Oh, I do so hope so!). Much salaaming and handshaking and we are gone.

Along the alleyway, through the gathering crowd of children wearing an extraordinary assortment of dirty western clothes from frilly taffeta dresses to falling-to-pieces cotton knickers. Back to the office. Back to the van. Back finally to the hotel where a feverish, slightly wild-eyed Adrian asks me anxiously, what was it like?

'It was all right.'

'All right?'

Yes, all right. It was all right. I wasn't talking about the living conditions that I had glimpsed during the afternoon. Or the exhaustion I had seen etched into the face of the thin, shy man who was Shahnaj's father. Or the dirt, or the poverty. I was talking about something that had happened to me on my inner journey.

You see, that afternoon God had allowed the veil to be lifted – and it was all right.

The final gate

A: I did say that illness has one or *two* positive aspects for me, and at the risk of sounding loony to some readers and perfectly normal to others (I'm not at all sure which of those extremes bothers me most), I would like to offer you a second example of this.

Occasionally, and particularly in the case of a feverish illness, there has seemed to be a small, peaceful place right at the centre of the vortex, where I am able to hear God speaking more clearly than at any other time. Yes, of course it may be nothing but my imagination, but I hope it isn't, and I don't think it is. And that is what happened when I woke or didn't wake or half-woke from that short but blessedly welcome sleep of mine, the one that began in the early hours of Friday morning.

Dimly I registered the fact that Bridget had left to meet Shahnaj without me. And this – this must be me left here, I reflected crazily. Yes, this was me stretched out on the bed like a giant piece of damp asparagus, dozing and waking and dozing and waking. What on *earth* was going on? At one point I caught my swirling brain wondering if perhaps the fault lay with British Airways. God had somehow failed to arrive with our flight from England, just as all our luggage had failed to turn up in Australia ten years ago when we took our first major trip abroad with a different airline.

Then, quite abruptly, but with an odd, artificial clarity, I found myself in that hushed, unstirring place I mentioned before, a place where good health and sickness alike mean nothing.

In front of me stood one of those heavy, white, five-barred gates, the sort of thing you find on farm tracks and at the edges of fields all over Britain. Somehow I knew, with that unchallengeably certain knowledge peculiar to dream-like episodes, that I would never be able to unlock this gate. Continuing along the path beneath my feet, one that for unrevealed reasons I was bound to follow, could only be accomplished by climbing to the other side. I was equally conscious, though, of being so hung about and weighted with bags and baggage of various kinds that, unless I abandoned at least part of my burden, the obstacle would be insurmountable. After a moment's pause I let one of my bags fall to the path, clambered awkwardly to the top of the gate, and dropped heavily to the ground on the other side.

I was made aware, without actually experiencing each occasion, that precisely the same thing happened with another five gates, each more difficult to negotiate than the one before, and each demanding that I discard more of my luggage. Then, as if I had reached the climactic scene in the sort of film that usually makes me cry, came the moment when I found myself standing in front of the seventh and last gate, a final hurdle separating me, as I now understood, from the place and the person that all followers of Jesus desperately hope to find at their journey's end.

One more gate.

If I could simply haul myself up to the top and lower myself down on the far side, all my travelling would be done. One more gate, the highest and most difficult of all to climb – impossible to scale in fact, unless I surrendered my sole remaining item of luggage.

When I tell you that this final piece of impedimenta turned out to be my relationship with Jesus and the security that I felt in my closeness to him, you will understand why my heart nearly failed me. It was all I had left, and a small, frightened child's voice inside me cried out that if I just dumped this last and most precious possession of mine there would be no point in going on anyway. It was a nonsense. And yet, according to the inner voice of my dream, I had little choice. I could settle for an eternally unfinished journey, crouching here for ever on the wrong side of this gate hugging my imperfectly fashioned images to myself, or I could more or less joyfully embrace the risk, hoping and believing that Chesterton was right in defining paradox as 'The truth standing on its head'.

I threw my last burden to the ground and began to climb ...

Probably just a dream, eh? But I would love to know if I made it or not.

• HAZARIBAGH •

A world of laughter

A: By the time I finally met Shahnaj on Monday I was feeling very much better. I *thought* I looked better. Now, though, as I flick through photos of myself on that day, I am horrified to see what everyone else must have seen. I closely resemble Barry Humphries' creation, Sir Les Patterson, a crumpled, almost lecherous-looking figure, apparently in the very early stages of recovering from a hard night on the bottle. Perhaps I had been more poorly than I realized. In any case, it didn't seem to matter.

As Bridget has already said, Shahnaj was the one with the light-bulb inside her. Her whole dwelling would fit into our sitting room four times, but her strong, sparkling personality would fill our house four times over. She was doubly special on this day because she was the main item. She was the reason for Bridget and me being here, and for the film crew being here, and for Sujit and Sanjay and Joanna and the other people from the project being here and for the gathering crowd of local people being here. She was a star.

One event in particular began the process which endeared Shahnaj to me. It concerned Sujit.

Sujit's journey to the slums that day had been less than comfortable. He was relegated to the back seat of the car, squashed into a corner against the window clutching an enormous globe of the world on a stand. The globe was bigger than his head and not much smaller than the whole of him. From outside the vehicle he looked like someone reluctantly employed as a deeply symbolic, living advertisement for the international scope of World Vision's work. In fact, the idea of bringing the object was that Shahnaj and I would sit in her house and look at the globe together. I would show her where Great Britain was, and then I would trace around the planet with my finger to show her where Bangladesh was. It would make a nice little bit of film.

Neither Bridget nor I were surprised when the globe fell apart after the baby grabbed at it, but at last we got the stupid thing under control and Bridget, Simon, Shahnaj and I arranged ourselves on the edge of the communal bed, ready to start filming. Shahnaj, easily as big a ham as me when it came to performing, had understood exactly what was required, nodding intelligently when it was explained to her, and was all ready to begin our 'spontaneous' little piece of interaction. It was just as Sanjay was about to say 'Action!' or something equally film-directorish, that she happened to look up and catch sight of Sujit in the corner of the room.

Sujit is a dear man, and I have the greatest possible respect for him, but only the most obtuse of human beings could have failed to understand why Shahnaj pointed, then leaned back and went into peals of laughter. The director of the film crew, anxious to get his lighting effects right, had asked Sujit to hold up one of those enormous circular reflector screens covered in silver foil. Sujit, who, as I have pointed out, is as unusually short as I am unusually tall, was standing obediently and solemnly in the shape of a star, legs apart, arms fully extended, holding this huge circular silver shape as high as he could reach above his head. He reminded me of one of those Victorian moral cartoons – feeble man straining to hold the moon

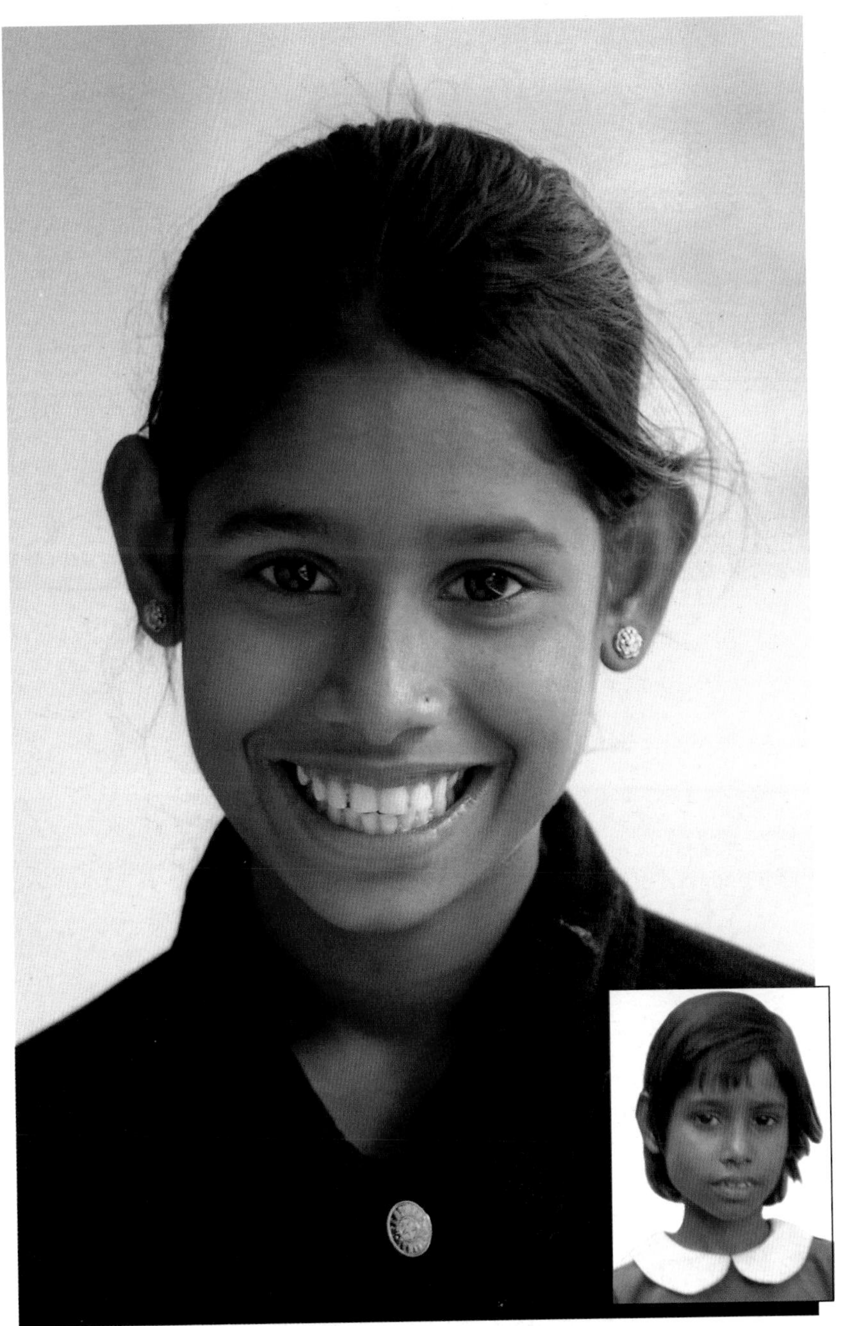

Shahnaj Begum, in the famous velvet jacket. (inset) Shahnaj, aged 6.

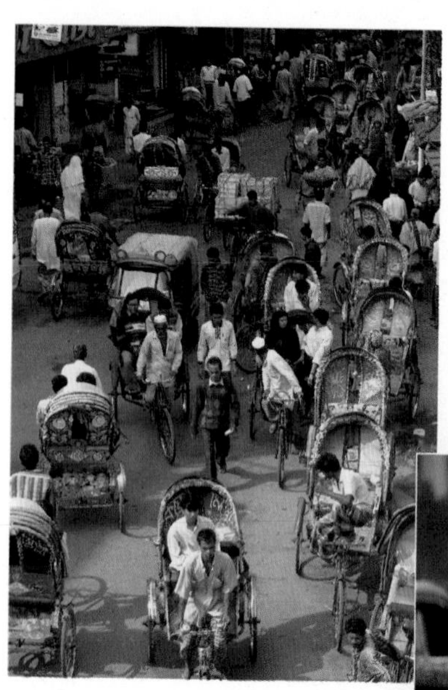

Dhaka traffic – a riot of rickshaws.

For a few taka more…

He didn't expect anyone to buy anything.

Planting rice.

River scene.

Father Parimal Rozario and his cow project.

The long and the short of it.

The Development Group.

In the slums.

Shahnaj at home.

Shahnaj and her class – just a tad camera-conscious?

Embroidery and friendship.

Dancing for visitors in the slum school.

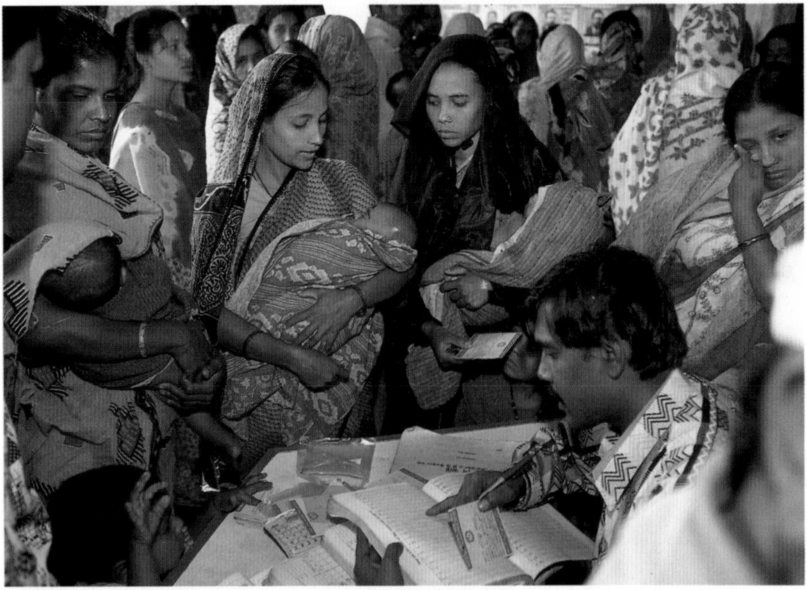

The health clinic.

Street girls and boys.

Scratching a living.

'Can street girls wear "nice dresses"?'

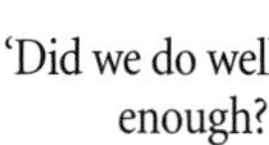

'Did we do well enough?'

Riding a rickshaw with our sponsor-child.

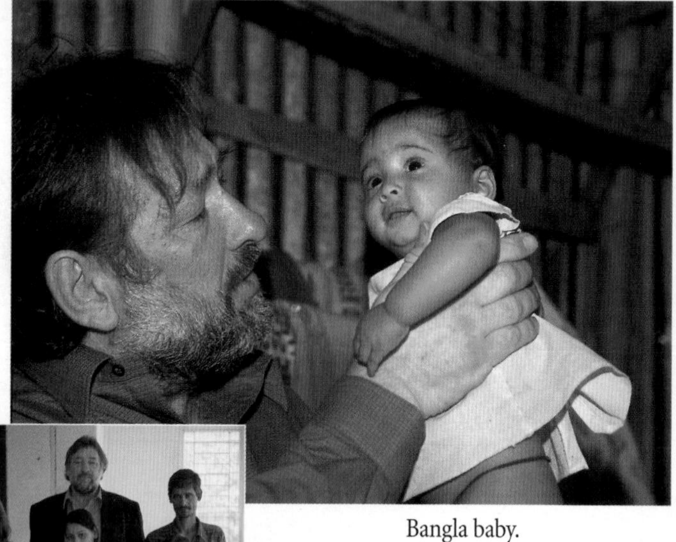

Bangla baby.

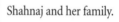

Shahnaj and her family.

aloft in his bare hands. The total effect was irresistibly comic, and I was no more able to resist than Shahnaj. I met her for the first time in the laughter we shared at that moment. Sharing a sense of humour is like two great rivers converging.

And Sujit laughed as well, thank goodness!

Light on salts

B: 'There's just one part of your gift to us we do not understand,' Joanna translates, while Shahnaj's mother eagerly burrows behind the makeshift curtain hanging from a baton on the back wall.

It is only my second visit to the family and, of course, Adrian's first, but the atmosphere is relaxed and we have been greeted by the children as if we are a favourite uncle and aunt whom they have known for years. It is a nice feeling. The rest of the family, perched around Adrian and me on the bed, smile expectantly and I confidently return their smiles, already in my mind planning how I am going to explain how to put together the decorative candle sticks, or reassure Suman that those Ferrero Rochers are for eating and not some obscure western-style jewellery to be attached to the earlobes.

After quite a lot of rummaging she emerges with a square of white crumbly dust nestled in mauve foil and holds it out happily. I stare. Helplessly I acknowledge inwardly what the family must have become instantly aware of, namely a certain added rosiness to my cheeks and neck. I am utterly overcome with embarrassment.

Still they smile. Still they wait. Still the outstretched hand containing the crumbling cube accuses me of rank stupidity.

'It's a bath cube.' I finally manage to force out the words.

'It's a bath cube,' translates Joanna happily.

'What do you do with a bath cube?'

Eager excitement from the Bangladeshi camp. Stunned silence from the English one. I see Adrian looking at me with horror. I interpret his expression:

How could you have been so stupid as to bring bath cubes to a family whose only access to water is a stand pump at the end of their street?

Inwardly I agree with him totally. How could I not have noticed that among the basket of soaps and gels that I had so confidently presented this lady with were two lavender-scented bath cubes?

Still they smile. Still they wait. Simon has a brainwave and excitedly whispers to her mother, demonstrating by rubbing it up and down her slender arm.

Joanna laughs.

'Of course – soap! Soap. Is it soap, Bridget?'

The pause seems endless.

Finally, carefully avoiding any eye contact with my husband, who I sense is keeping well out of the whole mess, I abandon any attempt to follow my conscience and own up to my silliness.

'Er, yes, it's a kind of soap. Sort of, anyway.'

'A sort of soap – soap, yes, of course it's soap. How silly of us.'

A chorus of happy chatter, laughter and apologetic head-shaking at their foolishness, as the precious cube is reverentially returned to its home behind the curtain.

Mortified, I sit in the midst of my lie and my cowardice, picturing the moment when our hostess, deciding to actually use my wretched present, finds her arm covered with gritty, lumpy, useless lavender-scented soda.

Perfect priorities

A: That same day we were taken to a walled yard where about fifteen very lively ladies were seated closely together in a circle on the ground, busily engaged on embroidery work. They seemed happy and chatty and bright as buttons.

Why did they need to meet in such an enclosed space, we wondered?

Well, because some of them needed to remove their veils.

And why did they include elephants in their beautiful embroidery designs? Was it because there are many elephants in Bangladesh?

Oh, no, there are hardly any elephants left in Bangladesh, but most of the customers for their embroidery want elephants, so elephants they must have!

And what did they all talk about as they sat and worked?

Oh, everything! News from their area. Problems that needed advice. Children. Husbands – much giggling.

What did this embroidery group give to each of them?

Money, one said. Work, said another. Friendship, said a third.

And which of these valuable things was worth the most?

No hesitation. The word for 'friendship' sounds from fifteen different mouths, filling the enclosed space, echoing from the walls and filling our hearts and the heart of God with pleasure. Oh, yes, friendship is worth the most!

The baby

B: The baby I had met and cuddled on my first visit turned out to belong to the sister of Noor Jahan, who lived next door. Perhaps fathers don't have a lot of time to cuddle small babies in Hazaribagh, especially baby girls. Clearly these two lovely women were amazed by the alacrity with which Adrian swept up their adorable pudding for a cuddle the moment she appeared. Anyone looking through our photos could be forgiven for thinking there was a never-ending line of identically dressed baby girls existing in every corner of the slum, because at every venue there she was again. Borne proudly by either Ragip or Simon she would be gently placed into Adrian's arms at any suitable moment, and at some extremely unsuitable ones as well. But he didn't mind. He's crackers about babies.

Shahnaj at school

B: From the first planning meeting it had been assumed that we would see Shahnaj at school. After all, education lay at the very heart of the child sponsorship scheme in Hazaribagh, and we had been looking forward to seeing her actually learning things.

I don't know what we had expected, but nothing prepared us for the stark reality of attendance at a government school in the slums of Bangladesh.

Hazaribagh primary school is an older building with the huge advantage that it is raised on pillars, and can thus double as an emergency centre every year when the floods come. There are four bare classrooms equipped solely with narrow wooden tables and chairs. No pictures. No colourful wall charts. No videos or televisions. No musical instruments. No gym mats. No apparatus. No craft materials. No carpet for storytime. No pots of felt pens or crayons. No displays of books. In fact, a blackboard in each classroom was the only aid we saw.

Walking the short distance from her home I had asked Shahnaj whether they learnt dance at her school. This question had produced another of her fits of giggles. At the time I thought she hadn't understood my question. Now I realized the giggles were precisely because she *had* understood! Her delighted amazement at the very notion of learning to dance at school reminded me of something else.

Many years ago we hosted a small boy from the East End of London in connection with the 'Children's Country Holiday Fund.' On the first morning our small guest stared open-mouthed and with obvious scorn at our boys liberally splashing milk into their bowls of cornflakes.

'Cor, do you use that stuff on yours?'

'Yes, why? What do you have?'

'Water o'course, you idiots.'

One man's milk is another man's water. As my father often says, 'It's all according.' Shahnaj didn't feel deprived because there was no dancing. She just felt normal.

The headmaster's teaching was disconcertingly abrupt, almost military in style. He rattled his questions off as though he was spraying verbal bullets around the room. The children caught them in their teeth and spat them back as answers. Leaping to their feet they responded immediately at the top of their voices in exactly the same staccato manner.

WHAT IS THIS?
IT IS A BOARD RUBBER!!
WHAT IS THIS?
IT IS A PENCIL!!
WHAT IS THIS?
IT IS A RULER!!

Presumably having run out of objects to identify, the teacher moved on to demonstrate his pupils' progress in their use of the English language. This was equally brief, and conducted at the same speed and volume.

SAY GOOD AFTERNOON!!
GOOD AFTERNOON!!
WHAT IS YOUR NAME?
MY NAME IS SIMA!!
MY NAME IS FATIMA!!
MY NAME IS SHAHNAJ!!
SAY GOODBYE!!
GOODBYE!!

It was hardly electrifying and seemed to lack any form of creativity, yet there was no mistaking the pride with which the teacher conducted his demonstration and the pride with which the children responded. Comparing notes later we discovered that we had both felt disappointed with the atmosphere of the classroom, especially when we compared it with the rainbow-hued ethos of the primary school in Hailsham that all four of our own children have attended. We needed to remind ourselves that education is a very serious business in Bangladesh, and also that the children were by no means cowed by their teacher's uncompromisingly stern manner.

'And,' said Adrian, 'it does mean she has a chance for the future. Thank God she's in a school at all.'

So we did.

Actually, there turned out to be a lot to thank God for in Hazaribagh. Look what has been established there with child sponsorship money just in the last two years. All those monthly fifteen pounds have been well spent.

What child sponsorship money was spent on in 1998 and 1999

Education

For everyone in the community:

Four pre-schools for 300 non-sponsored children, allowing mothers to work and preparing children for more structured education

Women's informal literacy classes run by World Vision-trained volunteers

For the 1,200 sponsored children:

Fifty per cent of school fees

Fifty per cent of text books

One hundred per cent of examination fees

School uniform once a year

Stationery and other materials twice a year

Special coaching classes to prepare for secondary school, high school and college exams

Spoken English classes for four months

Music classes

Debating competitions

Educational visits

Two sports days a year

Advocacy sessions for teenagers on their rights

Health programme

Curative

For everyone in the community:

Medical treatment at clinics three days a week (10,000 clinic visits in 1998)

Referral to hospital or other specialists of serious cases

For sponsored children and their families:

Full payment of all medical costs including hospitalization

Preventative

For everyone in the community:

Immunization for all under-fives against childhood illnesses
Immunization for all women of child-bearing age
De-worming for 8,000 people
Family planning for 700 couples
Annual health camp for treatments or referrals for eye, ear, nose and throat problems
Ongoing health education classes including nutrition
Six women's groups on hygiene and disease prevention
Three health workshops on primary health care, fifty local people attending each
Training for fifty traditional birth attendants (TBAs)
Leprosy clinic held twice monthly in collaboration with Leprosy Mission
Participation in national health days, e.g. Drug free day; Vitamin A day (capsules for 4,000 under-fives); polio free day (vaccines for 1,600 children); breastfeeding week
Provision of eighty-two slab latrines, each one to be shared between four families
Twelve new tube wells (several already provided)

Economic development

For everyone in the community:

Four new savings groups (103 women)
Revolving loan scheme disbursing the equivalent of £6,000
Training scheme in embroidery and tailoring for women
Doll making for teenage girls
Mechanics for teenage boys

Leadership development

For everyone in the community:

Teams of local people learning how to manage and oversee projects after World Vision has withdrawn
Three workshops for women on health activities
One workshop for TBAs
Meetings with teachers to ensure well-being of sponsored children

Training for project's pre-school teachers from Institute of Childhood Education in Dhaka
Training by World Vision Bangladesh national office staff for development workers

Relief

For everyone in the community:
Food and shelter at times of flooding

For sponsored children's families:
Four hundred blankets distributed during extra cold winter

Theatre – to go or not to go?

B: It was later on the Monday when I received my next massive jolt forward in understanding. As usual it was accompanied by a great deal of inward fussing and worrying, and as usual I had to learn that I was wrong.

We were back once again in Shahnaj's house, the programme for the day almost completed. All that was left was a little bit of film of Shahnaj pumping water, which must have seemed absolutely barmy to her – rather like saying to one of our children that we wanted to film them turning on the tap!

By this stage I really didn't care. All I wanted was five minutes break from being special guest to anyone at all, so that I could let my smile disappear for a moment and try to think of a few different superlatives. I was all too aware that I was beginning to sound like one of those plastic dolls, programmed with three different sentences which they repeat whenever the appropriate button is pressed or they are tilted in a certain direction.

Not that I hadn't meant any of it. Actually it *had* been a 'wonderful' experience, and I *had* found the embroidery work, the teenage toy-making and the tailoring class 'amazing'. It was just that Adrian whispering in my ear that he would kill me if he heard me utter these words of praise one more time had made me aware of the sparseness of my affirming vocabulary. Anyway, I comforted myself, the day had gone really well and Shahnaj, Ragip and Simon had had a ball, and were still full of energy and questions.

'Do your sons play cricket?'

'What does your daughter like to do?'

Just thinking about Kate made me wish she was with us.

'She loves to dance more than anything in the world.'

'I love dancing too,' Shahnaj said. 'I like Hindi dance. I have seen it on the television.'

Suddenly Sanjay's face appeared round the side of his camera. To be honest we were getting so used to the presence of the film crew that for a moment I had forgotten they were there.

'Don't forget I have a spare ticket.'

I had forgotten. That evening we were going to see an exhibition of dance at the National Museum Auditorium. It was part of a classical Indian dance week sponsored by the Indian Embassy, and Sanjay had suggested it as a way to unwind after the day's filming. He had procured five free tickets. To our delight and, I have to confess, surprise, Dhiman had expressed his love of classical dance, so the four of us were planning to make an evening of it, provided Adrian had not succumbed to the spotty fever again.

'You could take her to see some live dance. It will be a wonderful experience for her. She could come back to your hotel with you first.'

'That would be wonderful – amazing!'

No it wouldn't, it would be awful. How could we take her to the hotel? I would die of shame if she saw the ridiculous luxury in which we were staying, compared with her home. And how would she cope, and what would she eat? And what would happen if she saw life outside Hazaribagh? The only time she had been outside the area she knew was when she had accompanied her grandmother to the airport with her mother. Suppose it opened her eyes to the poverty she accepted as normal? How much good would that do her? How dare he suggest such a …

My express train of doubts and worries and fears suddenly seemed to have taken literal form as I became aware that I was physically on the move. The whole bed on which we were sitting was shaking as Shahnaj bounced up and down next to me, her lovely little face even more luminous than usual as she excitedly jabbered away to her mother and Joanna and Sanjay.

'But how will we get her home?' I asked feebly.

Apparently this was no problem. After all, was not Dhiman going to be with us? He would not mind. He would be pleased to help.

'Might she not be bored?'

Surprised laughter and shaking of heads from everyone once this was translated!

I acknowledged defeat but still felt very churned up. Was I right? Was I wrong? Was I genuinely afraid that to take her out of the bubble of the life she had known so far could affect her negatively, or was it myself that I was worrying about? Was I afraid that *I* was going to feel out of my depth? Would *I* cope? Might *I* never be the same again?

Until ten days ago Shahnaj had, in my mind, been a little child in a picture whom we were helping to feed and educate from afar. Now, I was taking her out for the evening to further her education and to feed her myself. My mind was still protesting that I couldn't possibly take my little starving millionth to the theatre. She was already getting much too real for my future comfort. I felt sick with anxiety.

Still laughing and talking the others went outside to finish filming as soon as possible so that there would be plenty of time to get to the dancing. I tried to pull myself together. What on earth would the evening be like? One thing was for sure – I would make sure she had a decent meal.

Dances with teapots

A: Of course, being a perfectly normal eleven-year-old girl, Shahnaj was equally determined that she would *not* have a decent meal. As our vehicle dodged and darted its way through the crowded twilit streets of Dhaka towards the theatre that evening, I turned to speak to her as she sat on the back seat, enjoying only the second car ride in her entire life.

Tonight, wearing make-up and dressed to the nines, she positively glowed with excitement and expectancy. This girl, it suddenly occurred to me, and her brothers and sister as well for that matter, could be transported straight into a British junior school, and within a week, leaving aside language problems, they would be thoroughly absorbed into the life of the community. Being loved and feeling safe in your own family are essential prerequisites for adapting to new circumstances, whether you come from Dhaka or Doncaster.

'Shahnaj,' I said, 'you must have something to eat on the way. You can have anything that you want – anything! Just say what you'd like most and we'll get it for you.'

Even at that stage, I must confess, a part of me still vaguely assumed that a child from the slums would opt for some kind of nourishing, well-balanced meal, rich in the right kinds of vitamins and nutrients, something calculated to stave off the pangs of hunger in more difficult days to come.

Yes, well – all right, I expect you think silly things as well sometimes.

There was no doubt about the enthusiasm of her reply when it came. She knew exactly what she wanted, and was not about to waste what might be the only fairytale-like wish of her life on anything as miserable as *sensible* food. Why on earth, when you think about it, would poor people want to make poverty their hobby as well as their full-time occupation?

What Shahnaj wanted was *misty doy*, a sweet, yoghurt-like confection widely enjoyed in Bangladesh by children and adults alike. In fact, Dhiman having located a little narrow shop on the side of the road that sold it, we all had *misty doy*, and I must say it was very nice. Bridget and I felt a bit guilty, though. We had promised to make sure she had a meal, and then given her the equivalent of sweets. Never mind, we reassured each other, she could have a proper meal on the way back.

Filled with anticipation and *misty doy*, we drew up outside the imposing National Museum building well in time for the seven o'clock performance. Alighting like rich people, we left Dhiman to find a parking place for the car, while we made our way up several grand flights of steps to the main auditorium where tonight's exhibition of dancing was to be performed.

Eyes wide with the thrill of it all, Shahnaj, impressed but not in the least overwhelmed, missed nothing. She took in the sweeping grandeur of the building, the expensively dressed, distinguished-looking patrons lining up before and behind our little party as we waited to be admitted, and at last, there in front of us, down at the far end of the raked auditorium, a wide stage softly lit with pastel colours, promising, as the theatre always should, the heart-gripping possibility that something magical – something impossible – is likely to happen.

As I took my seat next to Shahnaj I must admit that I felt more optimistic about something magical happening for her than for me. It is true that I have watched hours of dance because of Kate's involvement, but I don't always appreciate the finer points, to say the least.

Frowning, I adjusted my glasses and studied the programme that had been handed to us as we came in.

Hmmm ...

Tonight's event featured Sharmila Biswas and her troupe with something called an Odissi dance. Odissi, I gathered from my reading, was a classical dance style tracing its origins to the second century BC in a part of India now called Orissa. It was traditionally performed by Maharis or temple dancers before the images of gods. Tonight's presentation, called *Sampoorna*, was about the life of Mukta Mahari, caught between a rigid tradition that gives her a mysterious, goddess-like image, and the changing world which has very little place for her. Through the dances that we were about to see she discovers herself and the meaning of her existence.

Hmm ...

Sharmila Biswas, my programme went on to say, was dedicated to enriching and broadening the horizons of Odissi classical dance, and had participated in festivals and workshops all over the world.

Hm!

No doubt about it. This was going to be a class act.

By the time the presentation was due to start, the theatre was filled literally to overflowing. The buzz was very buzzy. For some reason the number of tickets distributed must have been far greater than the number of seats available. The sides and back of the auditorium were lined two deep with standing patrons. Even the aisles were packed to bursting. The atmosphere, to coin a phrase, was electric.

At last the house lights dimmed and the show began.

Now, Bridget has made me promise to communicate quite clearly and unequivocally the fact that *Sampoorna* was a highly skilled and deeply meaningful piece of work, executed with a degree of grace and dexterity that was entirely consistent with the very highest level of artistic achievement. She knows a bit about dance, so she's probably right. Certainly, as I learned later, Shahnaj and Dhiman understood and appreciated many of the finer points of the performance, and enjoyed it from beginning to end. The only problem I had was with the length of the production.

It went on for about a year, give or take a few months. A silly exaggeration, of course. It actually lasted for one hour and twenty minutes, which, coincidentally, happens to be the exact length of time that it takes the train to travel from Polegate, our local station in Sussex, to our nearest London station. In fact, in some ways that very familiar journey is quite closely paralleled by my experience of *Sampoorna*.

As usual I fell deeply asleep just after the level crossing at Berwick, woke with a start at Haywards Heath wondering how we could have progressed such a short distance in what seemed such a very long time, resisted the temptation to go to the toilet as we pulled out of Gatwick station, found the stretch from East Croydon to Clapham Junction grindingly, tediously interminable, and arrived at my final destination bleary-eyed and worn to a frazzle by sitting still for so long. My only consolation was that I didn't have to go back again.

As I have said, I'm sure that the performance was masterly. Yes, yes, the fault was in me. I do accept that. Perhaps if I had understood the symbolism a little better it would have helped. There was an awful lot of symbolism in *Sampoorna*. It was awash with symbolism. It was almost *all* symbolism. As it was, my responses to the things I did happen to notice each time the train stopped at a station, as it were, tended, I'm afraid, to be trivial or frivolous.

The periodic passages of English narration, for instance, were delivered in a voice eerily similar to that of Mystic Meg, the fortune teller who appears on a Saturday lottery programme on British television. A second important observation was that the principal female dancer, presumably the distinguished Sharmila Biswas herself, seemed to be made in such a way that the top half of her body was able to move laterally and independently of the bottom half. There are dolls like that. I believe they unscrew at the waist.

Then there were the men. These were far removed from the traditional western concept of the male dancer. Instead of being lean and muscular without an ounce of superfluous fat, they were on the verge of being – well – tubby. In addition, because of their bowed legs and the way in which both their elbows and wrists were bent at right-angles, there was what I can only describe as a strong teapot element in the shapes that most of them adopted while they were on stage. I am tempted to say that they poured themselves out for the audience, but – oh, well, I've said it now.

The end of the show was greeted with tumultuous clapping, thoroughly deserved, I'm sure. In fact, so loud and prolonged was the applause that it woke me up, and I joined in enthusiastically, immensely relieved to be pulling safely into Victoria at last. Looking along the row at the rest of our party I guessed from their animated faces that they had been happily wide awake for the entire journey – performance, I mean.

Before taking Shahnaj, still shining like a new star, back to her home in the slums, Dhiman dropped us off at Far Pavilions. One last thing to do.

'Take this,' I said to Dhiman, putting a 500-taka note into his hand, 'and make sure she has a proper meal on the way home, will you?'

'O-o-oh, yes,' he replied, masterfully confident, 'I will certainly make sure of that.' The next day I asked Dhiman about the journey home.

'Shahnaj did eat, did she?'

'Oh, yes, she ate.'

'Oh, good, what did she have?'

'Ah, well,' said the big man sheepishly as he handed me the change from my 500 taka, 'she had some more *misty doy*.'

Up until one

B: Of course, I realized during that wonderful evening how wrong I had been to worry, especially as we never actually had time to go back to our hotel, but two things that happened later confirmed just *how* silly I had been in trying to prevent this child from being as rounded and real as she undoubtedly is.

The first was when we heard from Dhiman about the *misty doy*. So much for my 'decent meal'!

The second was the next time we met the family.

'Did she enjoy it?' I asked Noor Jahan. 'The dancing, did she enjoy it?'

Although I now knew I had been wrong to worry about how she would cope with the experience, I think I was still deeply worried about the effect on her of seeing just how much brighter the world outside was.

'Oh yes,' came the rather dry response, 'she enjoyed it so much she was still telling us all about it at one in the morning. None of us was going to be allowed to sleep until she had told us every single detail!'

I started to apologize for the fact that she had not eaten properly and that she had kept everyone awake, but a twinkle in the eye stopped me. I felt the last veil lifting from my heart and drifting away for good.

I remembered vividly the first time I went up to London for the day with a friend's family. I had been the same age as Shahnaj. Part of the excitement was planning what I was going to tell everyone when I got home. Indeed, an essential ingredient of my happiness was keeping everyone awake until they too had experienced every single highlight of my day. Seeing the glamorous sights of London hadn't made me instantly dissatisfied with my comparatively uneventful life, any more than one night among the rich and elegant had affected Shahnaj. What a chump I had been! That special childhood day of mine had given me a tiny taste of spice, which meant that one day I would look for more flavour in my life.

Maybe her special evening will one day enrich her life in the same way. I do hope so.

• PROBLEMS FOR THE IMAGE-MAKERS •

A certain velvet jacket...

B: 'The problem is they all look pretty well, don't they – I mean they look far too well dressed.'

There was a tinge of worry in Adrian's voice as he looked over my shoulder at the prints I had just got back from the photographer's round the corner from the hotel. I understood his slight anxiety. Over the last few days we had witnessed extreme and sometimes horrific poverty. Yet here in my pictures was Shahnaj, smart in velvet, her brother Rajip clean and brushed, Simon naturally elegant, and Sumon self-consciously cool in shirt and curiously shiny trousers. They looked okay. As did the children we filmed in school and the women we met in their various groups.

Well, of course they did. They knew they were going to be on the telly! What would you do if you were told a film crew was coming to your house or your children's school? Would you decide to dress everyone in their dirtiest, most crumpled clothes and send them with filthy hair and grubby faces? Would you turn up yourself in your oldest clothes? Of course not. Ragip was probably scrubbed under protest like every boy under ten I've ever known. Simon will have probably begged her mum for a loan of her best scarf and as for Shahnaj and her velvet jacket – well, I'll come to that later!

Everywhere we went the women had made a huge effort to look their best and it was a joy to see, but this creates a problem for image-makers in the countries where funds are raised to enable the vital work to continue.

'All our research shows that huge-eyed, dirty children sell,' we were told by an acquaintance involved in promoting the concept of World Vision sponsorship in the UK, 'obviously people don't want to give their hard-earned money to folk who apparently don't desperately need it, however much you or I know they do.'

The problem was well illustrated by the business of the aforementioned velvet jacket. As I was careering around our house minutes before leaving for Bangladesh, I spotted a pile of clothes which Kate had recently outgrown and which was ready to be taken to our local charity shop to raise funds for the third world. On top of the pile was a much-loved jacket which Kate had reluctantly decided was just too small now. The irony of the situation did not escape me, and on impulse I shoved the jacket into my already bulging bag of small presents.

'You never know,' I muttered to myself, 'it might just fit, and I haven't anything for her that is actually from Kate.'

The idea appealed to me, but nothing prepared me for the awe with which Shahnaj took and stroked her secondhand present. When we arrived on the Monday morning she was wearing a traditional dress and looked very appealing. I could see that our cameramen were pleased. She vanished a little later, and on her return there was an almost audible gasp from the film crew as our diminutive star reappeared proudly wearing her new jacket and a pair of jeans presumably appropriated from her brother. No girls ever wear jeans in Bangladesh but Shahnaj knew she looked just like pictures she'd seen of western girls, and she was as proud as proud can be. And yes, she looked gorgeous, but she also looked utterly inappropriate. Even I could see that. But I could have cried, watching her face crumple as she was somewhat tersely told to go and change. I didn't really blame them. Time was money and we didn't have much of either to waste. About four minutes later she re-emerged in her school dress and now my sympathies went out to her mum, who stood looking very embarrassed behind her.

THIS DRESS WAS NOT CLEAN.

It bore a close resemblance to clothes which get to the bottom of my dirty clothes basket and remain there because I don't think they'll be needed for some time. It was not how she had pictured her little daughter being photographed. But I also knew that it was actually a truer image of the way these communities struggle to stay on top of filthy conditions in the slums, where their only aids to cleanliness are a cold water pump and a drying area on top of the corrugated iron roof of their houses. Pictures of this lovely little urchin in her crumpled blue dress were far more likely to encourage people in the west to give to these very needy children.

Shahnaj couldn't remain disheartened for long: Twice during the day she disappeared and returned hopefully wearing her jacket and jeans, to the laughter of the crew, who summarily dismissed her to change back into her school dress, which she did with increasing good humour. And she did wear them for her outing to the theatre with us that evening!

... and the case of the invisible telly

A: Well, it wasn't really an invisible telly, but we had to pretend that it didn't exist for the same reason that, as Bridget recorded, Shahnaj wasn't allowed to be filmed in her smart western clothes. You see, poverty-stricken people aren't really supposed or expected to have such things as televisions. Apparently evidence of such 'prosperity' is likely to have an inhibiting effect on potential donors to third world projects.

Is it possible that pity and power are linked in some sinister way when it comes to giving?

I don't know the answer to that faintly disturbing question. What I do know is that Shahnaj's family do indeed own a tiny, slightly battered looking black and white television set, one that the children have to be told to turn off when visitors come, just like children in this country. I also know, because we were told by that same advertising expert when we returned, that televisions are bad business when it comes to public appeals for new child-sponsors, and therefore it was better not to mention it.

I wonder if this is actually true?

Do the majority of people really align themselves with Margaret Thatcher, who publicly offered her view that the poor are only poor because they spend too much on cigarettes and beer? (She recanted the very next day, to be fair, but this time it came from the political mind rather than from the heart.)

Why shouldn't Shahnaj's family have a telly? Her older brother works in an electrical shop. He probably got it cheap or for nothing. Good for him. Why shouldn't they have anything within reason that might alleviate the grindingly impoverished situation that they live in and deal with day after day?

Well, whatever anyone else thinks, they've got one. Are you put off the idea of sponsorship by the thought that, in their six foot by six foot ramshackle house in a smelly slum in Dhaka, your child's family, led by a man who works twelve hours a day, seven days a week for a pound a day, might have a television, or a radio, or a ceiling fan or one electric light bulb? I'm not.

• CHITTAGONG •

The train

B: For some days since our return from Tuital a single thought had been clamouring for attention among the throng of ideas and thoughts jostling for position in my brain. It was a simple but persistent one. It was this.

I didn't want to go by bus from Dhaka to Chittagong on Tuesday morning. I didn't like what I had read in the *Dhaka Independent*.

> ***Death toll on the roads***
>
> *Road mishaps claimed some 27 lives in different parts of the country during the last few days. The types of accidents include overloaded bus skidding off the road into a ditch, train crashing against truck and auto-rickshaw, bus ramming into private car and auto-tempo as well as speeding vehicles running over pedestrians. Of the mishaps mentioned buses falling into ditches caused*

> *the highest numbers of deaths. In one such accident twelve people died when the jam-packed bus from Bogra to Dhaka met with a fatal fall as the driver lost control of the vehicle ... Witnesses observed that the bus was filled beyond capacity with passengers crammed on the roof top too. This is a common sight. It is observed that breaking of traffic rules by vehicle operators is more often the rule than the exception ... Of late death on the road mishaps has become so common that people are getting desensitized.'*
>
> Dhaka Independent, *Tuesday 18 January 2000*

I didn't like what I had witnessed for myself on the country roads. I didn't trust any driver other than Dhiman and I felt acutely aware that to take the risk of orphaning our beloved children by being fatally injured in one of these crashes would be extremely irresponsible. Hating to make a fuss, I was hesitant about voicing my growing anxiety, but fortunately Adrian agreed and Sujit was immediately amenable. A new plan was formed. We were to travel there by train and come back by plane.

Our train was due to leave very early in the morning and as we glided through the unusually quiet streets we witnessed a very different Dhaka from the frenzied, traffic-choked city we were getting used to. Everywhere was waking up. Carts laden with sleepy, silent women and children on their way to work moved slowly by. Little rubbish fires burned in the gutters as the street folk huddled in tiny groups to catch a little warmth after their cold night under plastic bag roofs. Shutters were being opened and street stalls set up. Nearing the station the bustle suddenly increased and I realized sadly that the beggars' early shift begins at first light. They were everywhere, displaying their various forms of mutilation like wares to be bought. As we got out of the car several children tried to act as our porters, while a young mother thrust her blind baby to within inches of my face. It is with considerable shame that I admit I was glad our available expenses stretched to first class tickets. So might you have been if you had read this article taken from a newspaper that I bought for the journey:

Train journey hazardous, passengers suffer

Passengers travelling on different railway routes in the district have suffered much due to lack of facilities on trains. The tracks in the lines laid during British rule have not been replaced ... The tracks have lost weight due to constant use ... and the pebbles are not found in many areas of the railway lines which are necessary to keep the railway lines in exact position. Most trains are running one or two hours late ... many passengers have to travel on the roof top or on the foot board at the risk of life.

Passengers complained that security guards ... regularly occupy good compartments forcing them to travel in inferior compartments. Railway employees occupy the seats and earn extra money by selling occupied seats to the passengers at a high rate.

Almost all compartments have no light, water, fans, doors or windows making the journey uncomfortable for the passengers.

The compartments become stinky with garbage ... left by passengers.

Some passengers carry goods like clothes, bundles and baskets of vegetables, drums of milk, fish and fish fry ... causing inconvenience.

Beggars move from one compartment to another causing difficulties.

Railways make heavy loss due to travelling by ticketless passengers. Ticket examiners also help passengers make the journey without tickets in exchange for money. There are therefore not enough seats for paying passengers because of this, causing inconvenience.

Dhaka Independent, *Tuesday 18 January 2000*

The second class coaches were already bulging with passengers, while still more were clambering on to the roofs as we strolled to the front end of the train. Our carriage turned out to be like something salvaged from the age of early English cinema, complete with brown leather seats and archaic metal ceiling fans, which whirred reassuringly when we switched them on.

Gathering speed we passed what must be the lowliest dwellings of all. Plastic bags covered with sacking stretched over the shallow embankment, with a selection of metal cooking pots and mattress bundles spread out to air on the disused railway tracks or on the dew-damp grass. Here and there a scraggy goat was tethered to a post.

Perhaps the most poignant image of all was the succession of minuscule allotments forming a patchwork along the edge of the railway line. Each sported a different crop. A few cabbages or cauliflowers or stalks of beans, even busy Lizzies, presumably to be sold on the streets to buy a little rice.

We began to move through the shanty town which has grown up on the edge of the city since the 1998 floods. Teetering on wobbling stilts, or made by stretching cloth over shaky bamboo frames, these homes had the stability of poorly erected card houses. They housed the people who were too impoverished even to afford the few taka necessary to rent a house in the slums. The filth, the piles of rubbish, the shocking sparsity of clothing, the dirty skins and running sores of the children who had stopped to stare at the train as it passed, horrified me, and I hoped against hope that something was being done to diminish the most obvious areas of deprivation. Sujit emerged from his newspaper to shake his head sadly in response to my question as to whether they had a project running here.

'World Vision works, as you know, Bridget, with the bottom ten per cent of our population, but we are responsible for the money which is entrusted to us. We cannot sink it into such a transient population. These people move on all the time. A project here is simply ...'

'Not sustainable.' I finished his sentence.

I understood. And yet I burnt with despair for those who fall below any percentages at all, who are simply non-people in the eyes of their country folk. Sujit seemed to read my thoughts.

'The thing is, Bridget,' he went on, 'we do not choose who will be helped. The community will themselves recognize they need help and will approach us. Maybe they have heard of our work with a neighbouring area. When we are approached we will send someone to that area to help them identify their need. Perhaps they will have a meeting in which they take paper and draw the things they feel are of most vital importance to their area. Maybe it will be through discussion. They will then commit themselves to supporting us as we put their scheme into practice, and to seeing it through until such time as they will be able to continue it for themselves. These shanty towns are too nomadic and not sufficiently organized to be able to participate effectively in a long-term project.'

Despite my swirling emotions I wanted to know more.

'So, who chooses which children will be sponsored?' I asked. 'Is it random, like picking a name from a hat?'

'No, it is not like that at all. The community leaders pick those children whose families will commit themselves to the programme's long-term benefits. You see, it will involve some considerable sacrifice for the family.'

'Sacrifice?'

'Oh, yes. You see the traditional way of thinking is that children are born to bring income into the family as soon as possible. Has it not occurred to you that Shahnaj, if she continues her education, will not be able to add to her family's income for many years, and this will cause hardship in the meantime?'

No, no, it hadn't. I thought of Shahnaj, and of Simon taking part in a six-month tailoring programme so that she could have a proper job later on. That family could teach me a thing or two about deferred gratification. I remembered how bewildered I had been on returning from seeing the toy-making programme which, I had been told, Simon attended, to find her feverishly helping her mother to complete her quota of tiny brown paper bags. Only afterwards had I put two and two together. Noor Jahan had sacrificed a day's work in order to make us welcome and was now frantically trying to make up time.

I hadn't really understood sponsorship at all. I had seen it simply in terms of people like us giving and people like them benefiting. Now I saw it in the form of an agreement between a variety of people, all of whom were committing themselves to a long-term plan in order to benefit a family and a community. There were people like us, for instance. We supplied the funds. But then there were the World Vision folk based at Milton Keynes who provided us with information, raised funds and ensured the safe passage of our money and gifts to their destination. Then there was the executive in Dhaka who took ultimate responsibility for making sure our money was properly spent on a viable scheme. They selected the right people to run the project and provided expertise and supervision. There were the local leaders, people like Joanna and Brownson, who took responsibility for running the programmes on a day-to-day basis.

And, last but not at all least, there were the parents of the children chosen. In our case, Noor Jahan, who had to make sure Shahnaj and Ragip got to school and availed themselves of all the opportunities on offer. Her overworked husband had to accept that his children would remain solely dependent on his income for the foreseeable future.

Sujit had returned to his *Independent* and nodded off. The sounds of his sonorous snoring and the loud Bangla singing coming through the speakers created a surreal soundtrack as I gazed out of the window at the increasingly verdant scenery. I was glad I had insisted on letting the train take the strain. Somehow, I don't think I would have been able to think through so much if I had been expecting to die every time we encountered another bus!

We passed through leafy, warm countryside, dotted here and there with comparatively prosperous farming communities, complete with haystacks, pecking fowls, chewing cows and playing children. It all helped to put the economic stability of the country into perspective, and I was able to relax and take pleasure in my surroundings. I was also, at last, able to set about solving the mystery of the paving slabs which had so intrigued me when I had seen them from the plane.

They were all to do with rice. The growing of the staple diet of Bangladesh appeared to involve several crucial stages and being there during the dry growing season meant that we were able to witness all of them.

First there was the nurturing to seedling stage. This was done in small square fields, which had been ploughed by oxen and irrigated from ditches dug around the edges. When the seedlings reached about eight inches in height and began to turn yellow they were pulled up and tied into small bundles. These fields were now redundant and, left without water, turned into slabs of baked earth – my paving slabs.

Now the seedlings had to be planted out into the paddy fields, and the sight of men, women and children, clothes hitched to their waists, bundles in hand, up to their calves in water, bending over and painstakingly pushing seedlings one by one into the mud in remarkably straight rows, was one of the most constant sights of our tour.

Elsewhere we would see fields which had reached the next stage, with the now established plants standing straight and green and tall and ready for harvest. The primitive irrigation systems, lengths of pipes tied together with thongs of jute, bringing water from the rivers to the fields was a reminder of the fact that water is always a problem to the people of Bangladesh. During the dry season, which of course we were in, absolutely no rain falls at all, but it is the only short growing season they have, and so it is essential that water be brought from the river to the field, however difficult that might be. When the rains come they don't stop for several months and if the harvest has not been gathered in it will be ruined. This is quite apart from the ever-present danger of flooding and cyclones. It didn't seem quite fair.

At last we arrived at Chittagong station, to be met by Liaquat Ali, a Muslim in charge of the World Vision work in Bakulia, a huge, desperate slum on the edge of the city. Tomorrow we would visit various projects, but now we were to eat and sleep. I settled comfortably into the back seat of the World Vision van and listened to Adrian trying to make sensible conversation with our new host.

LIAQUAT: I like hill area very much.
ADRIAN: (doing his D. of E. but sounding deeply puzzled) Oh, you like Hilaria very much, do you? (presumably thinking it's a Bangla band)
BRIDGET: (hissing in his ear) 'Hill area', you idiot!
ADRIAN: Oh, you like hill area very much, do you?
LIAQUAT: (who might be forgiven for thinking his visitor a tad slow on the uptake) Er, yes. Yes, I do.
(Silence while Adrian sinks into his seat. Sometimes there are advantages to being a back seat passenger.)

The monster of Chittagong

A: Our accommodation in Chittagong was owned by Christchurch, the centre for the local Anglican community. Perched high above the city, the colonial-style building surrounded by lush gardens enjoyed an air of bygone elegance that lifted it way above its modern function as a B & B. The air up there was sweet and clean. I slept well. Bridget didn't.

On Wednesday morning, just after stepping out of the shower, the process of drying myself was arrested when I suddenly noticed a small, handleless door let into the wall at the back of the bathroom. Inquisitive as ever, I wrapped a towel around my waist (just in case I was about to embark on some exciting ninety-minute Walt Disney-like adventure) and, forcing my plastic comb into the crack between the edge of the door and the wall, managed to prise the door open. Bending and peering tentatively into the dark and dusty interior of what I supposed must once have been some kind of storage space, I was unable to see anything at first. Then, as my eyes began to adjust to the darkness, I saw it – the monster of Chittagong. Motionless and menacing, it unflinchingly returned my stare from the far corner of the cupboard.

It was the biggest spider I have ever seen in my life. This awesome creature's body hung soft, bulky, satchel-like at the centre of a rope-like web, its legs, now twitching hungrily at the prospect of something extra large to pop in the larder, seeming to go on for ever and ever in every direction.

As it happens, I generally have no problem with spiders. They really don't bother me. Not that I would have been keen to cross swords with this one, I have to admit. This was definitely an arachnid to avoid. All I needed to do, though, for the sake of my peace of mind, was to simply close the cupboard door on my new friend and that would be the end of it. Out of sight, out of mind.

Now Bridget, on the other hand, cannot stand even the teeny-weeniest of spiders. They make her hair stand on end. One glimpse of the giant specimen in that cupboard would undoubtedly freak her out. Of course, there was the option of simply not mentioning what I had discovered. That would leave her free to enjoy the bathroom facilities without any fear that the beast of Chittagong might come bursting through the door of its lair to wrap eight hairy arms around her as she stood in the shower or sat in the bath. I did consider that option, but, do you know, in the end my conscience forced me to reject it. We Christians are commanded to tell the truth in love, so I did. I really loved telling Bridget the truth about that spider.

For some reason Bridget's next trip to the bathroom was extraordinarily brief. This person who had fearlessly faced a room filled with the poetic representatives of an alien culture with calm and confident assurance, came scuttling out of that bathroom as if she was being pursued by – well, by a monster.

A perfectly good field

B: 'Have you managed to get everything going you hoped for?'

We had been given a delightful breakfast by the World Vision team at their headquarters, and already we had gleaned a whole new harvest of facts about the area we were visiting.

Chittagong city is situated on the edge of the Bay of Bengal. As a consequence of two major cyclones in the last ten years, thousands of people in the surrounding rural community have been robbed of their homes and possessions. This has caused massive rural–urban migration, resulting in the slums being even more destitute than those around Dhaka. We learned that there were more than thirty slums with a combined population of over 600,000 people, and that Bakulia was one of the worst. Indeed, so extreme are the conditions of poverty, unemployment, lack of sanitation and illiteracy that a child survival programme has been instigated. Co-funded by World Vision UK and the UK Department for International Development, the 'Bakulia Health and Development Project' is due to end next year, so much of the present task is to make sure the work that has been done is sustainable (see how the word trips off my tongue) in the future.

??????? Did you know? ???????

One in ten children in developing countries are killed by diarrhoea and dehydration.

We were shown, in chart form, the aims set out four years ago. They were extremely ambitious. By 2001, all households were to have safe water. Community latrines were to be installed. Savings groups, education, sanitation, health education, immunization, pre-natal and post-natal care, family planning, safe fuel stoves – you name it, they hoped to ensure that the people living in this slum got it.

The list was a long one and as usual we didn't manage to take much of it in, but what we did grasp yet again was the passion and commitment of the team. We also picked up something else – a certain defensiveness. I was reminded of what Sujit had said in the train about World Vision being responsible for the money entrusted to them.

Liaquat looked anxious on hearing my question.

'Oh, no, not everything has gone as we had hoped. Sometimes we find that what we have planned in our meetings is not what the people actually want. Take latrines.'

Our preoccupation with toilets meant that he had a captive audience.

'Surely they want latrines, don't they?'

'We thought so, but we were wrong. There was much opposition, you see. Firstly we were told that they had a perfectly good field behind their houses as it was. Why do you need a latrine when you have a field? And secondly they didn't want them because it was up to the landlord to put them in, and if World Vision put them in the landlords would put up the rent and they were not having that. So no latrines.'

I made a mental note to refuse all cups of tea that day.

'What about the other side of the coin? Are there other things that have succeeded beyond your wildest dreams?'

'Oh, yes.' His sternly anxious expression vanished to be replaced by a positively beaming smile. 'Yes, I think you could say that. Wait until you see.'

To give to the poor ...

A: 'Now they would like *you* to sing a song to *them*.'

My heart failed me. Why should these poor children have to suffer more than they absolutely had to? Besides, what on earth could I sing that would have the slightest connection with anything that was familiar to them? What on earth ...?

We had travelled a street or two along the beam of Liaquat's smile, arriving eventually outside what appeared to be yet another slum dwelling. Stepping carefully through the low door we discovered that this windowless building, fairly dark inside despite being lit by a striplight on the ceiling at one end, had a quite different use. The floor had been swept clean and all furniture removed except for an easel against the wall beside the door. Cross-legged on sheets of matting spread around the ground, using their school-bags as little squashy desks, sat more than thirty primary-school age children of both sexes. The girls wore school uniform, a green dress, and most had their hair tied up with white ribbons, while the boys wore shirts of exactly the same green colour, hanging loose over a motley selection of patently non-uniform trousers. All were barefoot.

Arranged in neat rows to utilize the severely limited space, these bright-eyed youngsters were only slightly distracted by our entrance. Ninety-eight per cent of all available attention seemed to be firmly fixed on their teacher, a beautiful young girl in her very early twenties, dressed from head to toe in dazzling lilac, and exercising a warm, impressively commanding control over her small charges.

Looking round, we saw that, just as in an English junior school, the walls were covered partly with colourful posters, but mainly with drawings and paintings produced by the children. We asked the teacher if her pupils might be allowed to show us their individual pieces of work. One by one they stood to proudly point out the picture of a person or a kite or a house or a mango that was their own very special contribution to the classroom gallery.

'And what about you?' I asked a tiny child at the front who had not yet spoken. 'What is your name?'

'My name,' said the child, springing to his feet, 'is Saddam Hussein.'

Bridget and I exchanged glances. I'm sure we were both reflecting on the stark contrast between our mental images of the brutal dictator of Iraq, a man who had been known to summarily execute followers with a handgun when they displeased him, and this skinny little boy with huge, innocent eyes who was standing before us. We kept this reflection to ourselves, of course.

'And which of these drawings on the wall,' I enquired encouragingly, 'is yours?'

Walking as tall as his diminutive stature would allow, the little boy strode down one side of the classroom past two mangoes and a helicopter, turning left at a banana when he reached the end. Stopping, he pointed proudly with a forefinger, first at a pencil drawing on the wall, and then at himself, before drawing back modestly so that Bridget and I could approach closely enough to study his work.

'Ah,' I said, ready and willing to be warmly appreciative before actually knowing what the subject of his drawing might be, 'it's a ...'

'It's a handgun.' Bridget finished my sentence. 'It's a very detailed drawing of a handgun.'

Our noses almost met in front of the picture as we glanced briefly at each other again. Little Saddam Hussein had drawn a handgun. Oh, well ...

After that the children entertained us with dancing and music. Memorably, one little girl sang a brave solo as the rest of the class swayed gently in unison.

It was after this that one of the girls asked, through our translator, if I would now sing a song to them! I will charitably assume that Bridget was simply being helpful when she reminded me that one of the only things this class seemed to know about England was the story of Robin Hood. (They must have been very disappointed to find that I was not wearing a pointed green hat and carrying a quiver of arrows slung over my shoulder.)

'Sing them the Robin Hood song,' she suggested brightly.

'The Robin Hood song?'

'Yes, you know – riding through the glen and all that. Go on!'

I waited a moment for the Second Coming, but as usual it tiresomely didn't happen, so I girded my loins and sang the Robin Hood song:

Robin Hood, Robin Hood,
Riding through the glen,
Robin Hood, Robin Hood,
With his merry me-en,
Feared by the bad, loved by the good,
Robin Hood, Robin Hood, Robin Hood.

The thirty-six members of my audience greeted the end of this musical ordeal (theirs and mine) with wild enthusiasm, and then it was nearly time to go.

One last thing.

Bridget asked the teacher if there were any ways in which a child could be rewarded if he or she did a particularly good piece of work. The teacher shook her head – not really, no. Bridget produced a packet of little sticky-backed silver and golden stars that we had brought with us from England.

'We would like you to accept these as a present,' she said, 'to use in the classroom.'

There was no doubt that everyone was pleased, but, as usual, a gift without an exchange of gifts was as much an embarrassment as a pleasure for those on the receiving end. Teacher and class looked at each other dolefully for a moment. Then – inspiration! A bag was produced from a corner, opened and the contents tipped out on the floor. It was a collection of little models vaguely resembling animals and houses and people, fashioned by the children out of some kind of hard-drying clay or cement mix. These, the teacher explained, as her smiling class looked on and nodded in eager agreement, were to be our present from them in exchange for the silver and gold stars.

All was well. We left, clutching our bag of models and our new collection of memories, feeling that, all things considered, we had done rather well out of the deal.

As we walked away from that wonderful little classroom world, one which we enjoyed so much more than the government school in Hazaribagh, Liaquat described how community volunteers and teachers visit slum households to encourage parents to send their unschooled eight- to eleven-year-old children to classes such as we had just seen, as part of the non-formal primary education programme. Obviously the willingness of the project to provide a uniform and supplies for each child had been a huge encouragement in this respect.

Liaquat went on to explain that the kind of school we had just visited usually operates two shifts, one in the morning from 8.30 to 11.30, and another in the afternoon from two until five. Teachers are paid about fifteen American dollars per month, and are invariably women. A major advantage is that, because they live in the same community as their pupils, teachers tend to take a special interest in the welfare of their classes. Often, for instance, they will visit a student's home after school if a problem has arisen. Monitoring processes have shown these teachers to be competent, enthusiastic and well motivated.

We learned that many parents are pressing for the three-year programme to be extended by two years so that pupils can qualify to enter government schools that require five years of primary education as a condition of entry.

At the time of our visit a staggering twenty-two of these schools had been established. Eight were in their first year of operation and fourteen were in their second. And if I can offer you one more highly significant fact; of 773 students enrolled (two-thirds of whom were girls) we gathered that only 29 had dropped out. Evaluation has suggested that the quality of education in these programmes is considerably better than that provided in similar government schools. This is a truly great achievement.

Robin Hood supposedly stole from the rich. I don't think World Vision does a lot of that, but, in the area of education, quite apart from anything else, they are certainly giving to the poor. Perhaps all their workers throughout the world, and especially everyone at the Milton Keynes office, should wear a green pointed hat. In fact, God has just told me that they should ...

TBAs

B: 'Are we going to meet the ADPs after lunch?'

Immediately I knew I had said something silly. Next to me, Mary Dias, the doctor whom we had watched in action that morning, stopped making a little ball of rice and meat with the fingers of her right hand and turned to me in surprise.

'The ADPs? It is on our schedule, I think.'

Now the whole team had stopped talking and I was not surprised to hear a deep chuckle from the end of the table.

'I think you mean TBAs, Bridget. An ADP is an Area Development Project. I don't think we'll be meeting many of them after lunch.'

Sujit joined in the chorus of amused chuckling for what I considered a decidedly disloyal and prolonged length of time! I felt hot and miserable and uncharitable. I had hardly slept the night before. All morning we had witnessed the effects of poverty at close hand. We had walked through endless tense, tragically deprived, fly-infested streets. We had seen Mary hard at work in the filthiest, busiest health clinic imaginable, examining pregnant women in the scant privacy offered by a torn curtain. I had been hugged by a strange, elderly lady who assured me I looked just like her mother. We had heard the pitiful cries of infants being vaccinated. They looked too tiny and frail to be alive at all. Our hands had been wrung by a tearful mother who expressed hopelessness about the future of her little boy of eight whose right hand had been amputated after a firework accident during Eid. We hadn't been able to make phone contact with David and Kate at home for two days. I was tired. I was full to the brim with statistics and initials and poverty. I'd had enough.

Attempting to regain my position as interested spectator and to divert attention from my gaffe, I turned to Mary and asked in as controlled a manner as possible:

'What would you say was the most difficult aspect of your work?'

She paused again in her eating and seemed to consider my question seriously. Eventually she sighed.

'Absolute exhaustion, Bridget. I think that is the most difficult aspect of our work here.'

Looking round the table at these soldiers in the front line fighting against disease and disappointment I was utterly ashamed of my momentary slide into self-pity. I was going home in a few days. These highly qualified doctors, nurses and administrators had chosen to work in some of the worst conditions in the world for far less than they would earn in a government-funded post. Passion and commitment don't necessarily receive high material recompense. No wonder morale got low sometimes and the turnover of skilled staff tended to be higher than they would like.

'But, Bridget,' Mary interrupted my thoughts, 'we don't do it all on our own, you know. We couldn't. Our resources would never run to it and besides, as you know, our policy has always been to involve the community and to enable them to bring about change for the better themselves. The group you mentioned, the TBAs, are just such a group. And yes, you are going to meet them after lunch. We are very proud of them and of our work with them.'

So, a little later, there we were, drinking tea with some of the most trusted and respected members of Bakulia society. Without them the community would perish, for these were the Traditional Birth Attendants, or, as we would call them, midwives. Mary had explained that Muslim women are far too shy to go into hospital and would find examination by male doctors impossible. Almost all babies are born at home. When I thought of the conditions we had seen that morning I realized just how dangerous that must be for both mother and baby.

The figures I was shown in the project report confirmed my fears. The maternal mortality ratio is 224 deaths per 100,000 live births, and one of the main causes of death is what the project workers call 'referral failure'. In other words, women who have been referred to the hospital for specialized care just don't go, either because their husbands refuse to let them go, or because they can't afford the treatment.

Another frightening factor is the extremely young age of many of the mothers, victims of early teenage marriages. How dependent they must be on the skills of the TBAs. Yet, until the arrival of World Vision, midwives received no training at all, either in basic hygiene or in methods of delivering babies safely.

Looking through the report, though, it was not all bad news. When I compared the national average of infant deaths (a horrifying 71 to 82 deaths per 1,000 live births) to that of Bakulia (22 per 1,000), I realized that something exciting was happening, and that the secret was right here in this room.

There were fifty-two of them. They didn't exactly look like heroines. They were all older and rather more weatherbeaten than most of the women we had met. In fact, in all honesty, both Adrian and I thought they looked a bit rough round the edges! But they also looked tough. And strong. As if they'd seen it all and found ways to cope in the direst circumstances. Exactly what you need if you are a frightened teenager giving birth on the floor of a tiny room with no water, no sanitation and probably no electricity, in the middle of one of the worst slums in the world.

Sitting on rows of benches in one of the rooms at the regional centre they were being instructed by one of the qualified nurses we had met at lunch. She was looking through a pile of forms covered in pictures, glancing up every now and then to say something or to smile at one of the women. The atmosphere was relaxed and the response confident. They were clearly more than happy to answer our questions.

Yes, it was true that until a few years ago they had received no training and they hadn't understood how important it was to have everything very clean. Yes, they were all trained now. Twenty-two days training covering hygiene, recognizing and referring obstetric problems, and safe-birthing techniques. They had learnt how vital it is to promote breastfeeding and for mothers to take vitamin A after the birth. They had been encouraged to refer their clients for immunizations and ante-natal and post-natal checkups.

As our translator struggled to keep up with the energetic and competitive responses, and attempted to make himself heard over the bedlam, I remembered what Mary had said about the professionals not being able to do the job of bringing about improvements in healthcare on their own, and realized how true this was. These women alone commanded the trust and respect needed to persuade frightened, modest mothers-to-be to submit themselves to examinations and to convince them of the importance of vaccinations.

There was one piece of information they were all anxious to convey. At the end of the training they had all been presented with their kit.

'Your kit?'

Loud discussion was followed by the exit of one of the women, who returned carrying a small case which was passed over heads to the front and opened for our admiration. There was a small saucepan to boil the water to sterilize the razor blade which they proudly told us had now replaced the sharp piece of bamboo they once used to cut the umbilical cord. There was cotton wool and soap in a soapdish, and a plastic nailbrush so that they could scrub their hands before delivering the baby. Then there was more cotton wool, plastic gloves, a plastic sheet, Dettol, and gauze bandages to help ensure a safe delivery. Oh, yes, it made them feel very proud to know that they were trained, and much more confident to feel that they were properly equipped to do a professional job.

And would we like to see the charts which they had to fill in and present at their weekly meeting?

We certainly would.

Now I understood why the forms were pictorial, with a box for keeping a tally chart. Hardly any of our heroines would have been able to read or write. On the charts, which we had seen the nurse discussing with the women when we joined them, every pregnancy was recorded. Boxes to be filled in included whether the TBAs had passed on information about the importance of a nutritious diet, health, rest, immunization and ante-natal care. Then the birth, the cutting of the cord, any hospital visits, and for the baby, sight and hearing test. A check on freedom of movement had also to be recorded. The TBAs now fulfilled the role of health visitors as well as midwives. No wonder they were proud of themselves.

Was there anything they were not happy with?

Yes, there was. They would very much like to be paid.

What were they paid at the moment?

Oh, little gifts from the families. Usually soap. Or rice. But now they were trained they felt they deserved a little more.

You bet they did, and I must confess I felt quite angry that World Vision had not seen fit to pay their staff. We vowed we would address the problem, as we saw it, before leaving Chittagong.

First, though, we were off to the seaside.

A strong tower

The name of the Lord is a strong tower.
The righteous run into it and they are saved.

B: I remember once seeing that song beautifully illustrated by two deaf members of a huge Baptist congregation in South Africa. Their faces alight with passion and confidence, they portrayed the truth of those words in sign and dance. Now, standing in considerable awe on the roof of the cyclone rescue shelter in Patenga, an area near

Chittagong, I experienced an even more concrete (forgive the pun) illustration of this truth.

Over the past 180 years there have been no less than two hundred cyclones, six of which proved so severe that over fifty million people lost their lives. Looking down through flourishing palm trees to mile upon mile of green, sunny fields it was almost impossible to believe that in 1991 a freak combination of weather conditions produced the worst cyclone this coastal area had seen for many years, quite literally wiping out everything in its path. Devastating in itself, this violent twister churned up the sea's surface so violently that it was followed by a tidal surge fifteen feet high. I cannot think of anything more frightening. To cling for hour after nightmare hour to something barely strong enough to hold your weight, sick with fear, ducking the debris, the dead animals and corrugated roofing this monster wind is hurling in all directions, your mouth dry with salt, is bad enough. To look up and see a wave fifteen feet high striding towards you is beyond description. Yet that was the experience of many village folk we had met that afternoon.

Every one had a tale to tell. They showed us the flimsy corrugated roof where an unbelievable six hundred people had clung for several hours while the waters swirled over them. They talked of the horror of ruthlessly scrambling over each other to try to gain a few feet of safety for themselves and their loved ones. A grandmother told us how she had sheltered her four-year-old grandson with her body. A mother, how her little girl had disappeared for ever into the dark frothing waters, and of strange fireballs some of them had witnessed bouncing on the sea.

It must have seemed like the end of the world.

They told us of the horrors waiting for them as the wave finally lost its appalling strength and the wind passed, of the darkness which descended on their little world for several weeks as all electricity supplies were rendered utterly useless. They talked about the dead, bloated livestock which floated on the subsiding waters, some showing inexplicable burn marks. They shook their heads over the tragic demise of their fragile homes, most of which had collapsed completely. All their household goods gone. No clothing. No bedding. No food. No unpolluted water. No roads to escape on even if they had something to escape in.

??????? Did you know? ???????

7,000 arsenicosis patients have so far been identified in Bangladesh, while 63% of tube wells contain unacceptable levels of arsenic.
Dhaka Independent, Monday 17 January 2000

And then they talked about World Vision: about the boats arriving with parcels of rice and bottled water, blankets and even cooked food. And hope. Hope that life would go on. They had not been overcome. There really was hope, hope symbolized by the extraordinary structure on which we were now standing.

I can only do my best to describe it to you. Several stories high, it's built in the shape of an arrow head, the point directly facing the Bay of Bengal. The two sides are divided into large numbers of small rooms equipped with metal shutters designed to withstand the very worst this volatile climate can throw at them. At intervals along the walls, painted in huge letters and illustrated for the non-reader, are a series of instructions clearly numbered one to ten, which can be seen daily by children on their way to school and by adults as they make their way to the market and to work in the fields. The shelter is linked by telephone to the weather centre in Dhaka, which monitors all weather changes and reports as soon as any danger is imminent. Then a megaphone comes into operation in the hours before disaster strikes, booming out the numbers at regular intervals to the surrounding villages.

Number one means that there is a possibility of a cyclone over the next twenty-four hours. I'm not too sure what two to four mean (the writing was all in Bangla) but number five indicates that it is considered unwise to leave your village. Number six advises communities to dig a hole and bury their supply of rice under ground, leaving some clear indication of where it is hidden so that when they are able to return to their homes they have immediate access to a food supply. Number seven means leave everything and come to the shelter bringing only your animals with you. I suspect numbers eight, nine and ten are increasingly urgent messages on the same theme. What I do know for sure is that the system has been tested and proved successful twice since it was constructed after the 1991 disaster. Three thousand people on two separate occasions have streamed over the fields to take refuge in this one shelter, and World Vision have built fourteen of them along the coast.

Of course, they are not alone in their determination to provide cyclone shelters, but they are responsible for the unique shape of their buildings. The arrow points, as I have said, towards the sea and as the twister gathers force and speeds towards the shelter that point is directly in line with the eye of the storm. At the moment of contact between these two Titans, the wind is literally sliced in two, and its power dissipated as it rushes along the length of each side of the building, quickly losing the worst of its horrific power. Naturally, there is still going to be devastation, and whole villages are still going to be wiped out, but no lives have been lost in this area during flood or cyclone since the shelters have been built.

A little story you might like. World Vision workers are not allowed to evangelize, but in 1998, while the ITN crew were there filming the crisis, the team produced a hot meal for all those staying in the shelter, and, as usual, prayed over the food before distributing it. A respectful silence fell on the all-Muslim queue, and indeed on the ITN reporters, as thanks for the food and for the rescue of all those about to receive it were offered to God.

As one worker told us with awe in his voice, 'After that it felt like administering communion, so blessed was the atmosphere.'

When the big bad wolf comes we'll be ready – with a bit of wire

A: Have you seen *Titanic*? One scene chilled my blood. It's the one immediately after the collision with the iceberg. Urgently needing to estimate the likely effects of the damage, Captain Smith, his chief officers and the designer of the ship are studying plans and diagrams depicting the great liner's series of supposedly watertight holds. Almost immediately they are forced to conclude that their ship is doomed. This terror-filled moment is intensified by the bizarre contrast between barely contained horror in the voices and expressions of this small group of men who know the appalling truth, and the fact that, for the time being at least, the so-called 'unsinkable' liner is floating quietly on the calmest of seas under clear and starry skies. Later the surviving passengers must have asked themselves how it was possible for such serenity to be the prelude to such cataclysmic disaster.

Climbing to the top of the arrow-shaped Cyclone Centre that Bridget has described so vividly, and gazing out at well-ordered villages and green fields stretching endlessly away into the distance, I remembered that *Titanic* scene. Behind me, vast, ancient and, to my limited perception, part of a mysterious, almost mythical eastern world of which I knew nothing, the Bay of Bengal was once again biding its time. Soon, perhaps only in a couple of months from now, the huge shoulders of yet another cyclone would raise themselves with unbelievable power from that dark place, seeking, like the big bad wolf who had frightened me out of my skin when I was a small child, to huff and puff and blow this World Vision concrete house down.

'May he be as unsuccessful next time as he was last time,' I prayed quietly.

And all God's little pigs said, 'Amen!'

They did. I heard them.

'Come and see what the wind did last time,' our guide called from farther along the roof. 'Look down there.'

I peered over the low parapet that ran round the edge of the roof. Far below us, a shed or outhouse at the back of the Centre had suffered quite serious damage. There was a big hole in its roof.

'It looks as if something's fallen on it – something really heavy,' I guessed intelligently.

'Yes,' replied our host, 'it was during the last cyclone.'

Straightening up and turning, he administered a couple of brisk slaps to a truly enormous concrete slab resting on top of what seemed to be a chimney of some kind.

I stared incredulously.

'You're not seriously telling me that—'

'Lifted it like a kite,' he said, 'and dropped it straight on to the roof of that building down there. We had to hoist it up and put it back.'

'But won't the same thing happen again next time?'

'We've fixed it – look.'

He pointed to a short, scrappy little length of rusty wire, attached to the slab at one end and the base on which it rested at the other. I studied it in silence for a moment, then, quite unable to contain myself, burst into laughter.

'I'm sorry,' I spluttered, 'but are you seriously trying to tell me that when the cyclone arrives, licking its lips at the thought of another round of slab-chucking, it's going take one disappointed look at that wire, and say, 'Oh, no! Look what the spoilsports have done. They've fixed it on with a bit of rusty wire – now I won't be able to play with it', and then slink off back to the Bay of Bengal to sulk?'

There was a pause. Slight worry. Do laughter and Cyclone Centres ever mix? Yes, well, they did this time anyway, thank goodness. Everybody laughed.

I remember that tiny token of resistance with a sort of affection. It reminds me that even the largest and most ambitious projects come down in the end to ordinary people doing their best and trusting God for the results.

David against Goliath, Gideon against the Midianites, Job against twittish friends, the widow's mite against a world of need, a scrap of wire against a cyclone – nothing changes much, does it?

To pay or not to pay

B: After we had said our goodbyes and returned to Bakulia we both felt we owed it to the TBAs to raise their grievance. Sitting and drinking tea with Liaquat and Mary seemed a good opportunity.

After all, surely the facts spoke for themselves. Not only were more and more babies being delivered safely, but the number of newborn babies being exclusively breast fed and then receiving necessary complementary feeding from five months, and the number receiving vaccinations, had all risen in the last two years by about twenty per cent.

'You need to understand,' explained Liaquat, 'that proud as we are of our involvement with them – and you are right, we certainly could not do our work successfully without them – they are not our staff.

They have always belonged to their community and they still do. Naturally they should be paid properly, but if we began to think of them as our employees we would immediately create a problem, especially when we withdraw over the next two years to start another project elsewhere. Of course we want them to continue to put into practice all they have learnt, and we hope that basic training will be considered essential in the future. We also hope that the community will understand that they should pay properly for the services they receive. But however grateful the family may be, it is often too poor to give more than they do at the moment. A little rice given away may mean the family missing one meal. Our women's savings groups are already being encouraged to put money by for obstetric emergencies, and that may be the way forward. Also work needs to be done with Chittagong city corporation. Our proposals for effective phasing out of our work here include meetings of the Bakulia community with civic, social and public health leaders, so that the health programme will be sustainable without outside resources.'

When we finally left the office that evening and headed back slowly through the clogged rush-hour traffic to the comparative luxury of our sheltered hilltop guesthouse, we all felt a little overwhelmed by the sheer volume of need and rescue we had witnessed that day. Sanjay clearly felt we needed cheering up.

'You know the little boy we met this morning called Saddam Hussein? Well, the decision his parents made to call him after a famous person reminded me of a man I met in Cambodia. He told me he had three sons. One was called Alexander, one was called Mussolini and the third was called Hitler. I just had to ask him why he had decided to call his youngest son that.

'"Ah, well, you see," the man told me, "when I was a young man I was a soldier, and at that time Hitler was a very, very famous man. I do not know why, but his name was in the paper every day. I saw it everywhere. The name Hitler. Oh, yes, he was a very, very famous man. You are only young. Too young to have heard of him but at the time he was a *very* famous man."'

• STREET GIRLS •

Being a girl

B: Before we talk about the street girl project, let me tell you what we have learned about the general issue of simply being a girl in Bangladesh.

When our daughter Kate was born thirteen years ago it was a day of vast celebration. After three boys we had at last been blessed, a little unexpectedly, with a lovely little girl. I can remember our predominantly male household, one in which the boys' bedroom walls were covered in football posters and their cupboards filled to bulging with cricket pads, footballs and skateboards, being temporarily turned into a shrine to girliness with pink cards and flowers and bows filling every available space.

Customs vary from country to country and culture to culture but the birth of a girl child in Bangladesh can still mean a shaking of the head and a sighing acceptance of the bad fortune bestowed on the family by Allah. This is symbolized at the female infant's naming ceremony by the sacrifice of only one animal as opposed to two for a boy. For the strictest Muslim families her inferiority and lack of independence will be reinforced by the religious instruction of 'purdah', which literally means 'curtain' or 'veil'. When a female child reaches her teenage years she is only allowed to venture outside her family home if veiled in a 'burkha', a dark garment which envelops every inch of her body except for a slit or two holes for her eyes.

This doesn't mean that her father, or later her husband, are necessarily cruel or insanely jealous. Men are taught that if they do not prevent their women folk from moving freely their names will be written in the book where sins are recorded, and they will be doomed. This horrific obstacle to the development of women is, sadly, man-made. Although the holy prophets stated clearly in the Qur'an that both men and women should be educated, because of the veil women are not allowed to be taught by local religious priests nor to attend meetings, festivities or even to enter a mosque. There seem to be Pharisees in every religion! This means that many women are not allowed to participate in economic activities outside the home, and thus cannot contribute to the family income. All in all it is not surprising that female children are considered a liability and a burden, and that their arrival is not greeted with a fanfare. This is especially the case when all the rites associated with marriage are added to the equation, because here as well, having a male child is a huge advantage.

According to Islam, marriage is compulsory for every man and woman. Presumably in order to make sure this rule is taken seriously, Muslim fathers in Bangladesh with unmarried daughters are not allowed to make a holy pilgrimage to Mecca. No wonder the parents of girls are anxious to arrange the marriage of their daughter as early as possible, sometimes even as young as five. Arranged marriages are the cultural norm for not only Muslim but also Hindu and even many Christian families in Bangladesh. Traditionally, first the boy's guardians will approach the girl's guardians via a go-between who establishes the suitability of the marriage in broad terms. Is the girl younger than the boy? Is she shorter? Is she less educated? How dark is she (pale is beautiful)? Is she strong? And last, but not at all least, can the family afford what the boy's family are asking in the way of a dowry?

If all these aspects seem satisfactory (though how on earth you can tell if the girl is going to outgrow her future husband at the age of five is beyond me!) the boy's mother will come to see for herself, followed shortly afterwards by the father, who will make a formal approach. Finally, the boy himself will arrive accompanied, like Rabbit, by his friends and relations, and the girl will serve them tea and answer any questions he has for her. If she pleases him word is sent from the boy's family to the girl's that they have agreed to take her.

Sadly, things won't necessarily improve for the girl after marriage, as her husband takes over the traditionally dominant role from her father. According to Islam a woman can only get into heaven if her husband is satisfied with her in all respects. She is expected to be devoted and obedient and to listen to her husband without protest, touch his feet and never call him by name. And it is not just her husband she has to please.

After the wedding the bride and groom leave the bride's house where the ceremony has taken place at huge cost to the bride's family, and move into the groom's house where his mother takes the bride's arm and leads her in. Now the wife must also please her mother-in-law, and if she does not come up to expectation can expect to be beaten and punished. Worse, she can be divorced at any time and without any reason, leaving her to face economic disaster, either returning to be an extra, unwelcome burden on her father's house, or facing life on the streets as a beggar or a prostitute.

One of the main reasons for divorce is that the dowry has not been fully paid by the bride's family. Although essentially Hindu in origin, the dowry system pervades Bengali culture and has become an increasingly widespread social problem. Even Christian women face similar problems with the dowry. Demands have increased so much that the bride's parents often get into heavy debt before the marriage. The poor little wife will often be beaten and sent back to her family with fresh demands for more money, even if the original dowry was paid, reinforcing the parents' negative feelings towards girl children in general and their own in particular.

Thankfully things have started to change, partly due to government initiatives. (This is reflected in the surprising fact that both the prime minister and the leader of the opposition are women.) However, in a society where the prevalent cultural myth is that women are by nature physically weak, intellectually poor, mentally inconsistent, timid, irrational and psychologically unstable, change at grass-roots level could take some time! Especially when the myth is reinforced not only by the male members of society, but also the females who accept their inferiority as the norm, a fact which came through very clearly in a survey, 'The Girl Child in the Family and Society', sponsored by World Vision in 1993. The sample used was a total of 150 very poor households from both rural and urban areas. The 'son-preference syndrome', as the survey charmingly called it, showed that girls were more likely to suffer diseases and more likely to be malnourished because the men and boys would be served first and given the best quality and quantity of what little food there was. Women were found to be mostly ignorant of any rights, and therefore not able to encourage their daughters to stand up for themselves in any way.

By law girls are not now supposed to marry until they are eighteen, this being one of the government's attempts to bring society into the modern era. Yet in the sample households thirty-six teenage girls were married, two of them in the age group 10–14 and thirty-four in the age group 15–18; hardly any of the households that took part in the survey had even heard of the prohibition of marriage under eighteen. As far as most were concerned puberty was still the ideal age to marry off the girls if only to prevent them being 'spoiled'.

The survey showed that these young married girls were frequently physically and mentally tortured by their in-laws, and often sexually abused outside the home. Of these, two had been divorced and seven separated or deserted before they had even become teenagers. In almost all cases it was found to be non-payment of the dowry that was the cause. The survey found that none of these young girls had any knowledge of rights they had by law. They didn't know, for example, that the practice of divorce by the husband uttering 'I divorce you' three times is not legally valid. Or that they have the right in certain circumstances to divorce their husband. Or the right not to be subjected to torture at the hands of their in-laws. They remain victims of their own ignorance and helplessness and clearly will continue to do so unless someone, somewhere takes the initiative to bring about change.

Violence against women

Masculinities and Violence against Women
by Dilara Chowdhury

The violence against women in 1999 according to this report (Odhikar: Dhaka Human Rights Coalition) had been steadily on the rise. 835 women raped. 10 by police. 75 women died as dowry victims. 153 women sustained burn wounds. The saga of violence against women was epitomized by the highly publicized assault on a young woman at Teacher Student Centre at Dhaka University in the presence of hundreds of young men and law enforcing agency. The nation should hang its head in shame at the fact that it had taken place in a university campus thought to be the sanctuary for the victims of all injustices … in reality what transpired so far were a few pieces of articles in the newspapers … no outcry, no sense of shame, no sign of remorse on the part of either our political leadership or leaders of our civil society … A mindset immersed in the belief that men are naturally masculine propagates aggression in men and their association with violence. In reality it is a cultural construction. Social practices that associate men with violence … are rooted in the writings of ancient and modern political theorists, so called findings in hormonal testosterone levels, sociobiological readings, religious sermons like the Chokhbazar Hadiths and versions of history in which men are socialized to be aggressive for the survival of the species. Our cultural environment permits an all pervasive tendency to put the women in the dock whatever the situation might be. Hence the female students of Jahangirnager university were thought to be responsible for inviting rapes because of being out in the campus at so called odd hours and by not dressing properly.

The victim of TSC assault also facing criticism. Most do not realize that it was her right to be there to celebrate the coming of the millenium along with other citizens … The underlying message is that she should not have been there because she was not following men designated social and cultural norms and had the audacity to be there. The remedy lies in the willingness of the men to change in their moral intellectual outlook or in their psychic-social behaviour.

Dhaka Daily Star, *Tuesday 18 January 2000*

Acid throwing

Letters to the Newspaper: Victims of Acid Throwing

Sir,

The state of our country seems to have reached a sickening height where crime simply goes on and on. Frustrated young men ... began the abominable practice of throwing acid on young women who did not respond to their advances. Rebuffed but never daunted these young men ... would creep near the window of the young ladies and when they were in bed fast asleep, cruelly ruin their slumber and shatter their lives by drenching them with acid. I do not know what punishment can be devised that can fit the crime committed ...

Mesbahul Akhtar Dhaka

Dhaka Independent, *Monday 17 January 2000*

After reading the survey and articles like these, we began to understand why World Vision see their work with women and girl children in Bangladesh as being of paramount importance.

The nice dress

B: Of all the information Adrian and I had been given before we left England there was one report which intrigued us above all others. It was the report on the street girl project in Dhaka city. Having worked with children in care for so many years this project had immediate interest to both Adrian and me, and when we discovered it was not on our schedule we asked if it could be fitted in.

Adrian's illness had naturally made the possibility of this extra visit difficult, but by flying back from Chittagong instead of coming by bus we had released several valuable hours.

So, here we were, and I had to confess to being rather disappointed. We were sitting in yet another office, looking at yet another complicated chart showing staff structuring and sets of aims and achievements laid out in percentage form, with a small, rather severe woman called Lufte Tahera, who read out the information from the chart projected on to the wall in a dry lecturing tone, as if we were unlikely to be able to read it ourselves.

'Do you have any questions?'

Feeling like students at the end of a heavily factual lecture, we racked our brains somewhat dismally, not wanting to show ourselves up. All I could think of was something which had fascinated me ever since I first looked at the information pack in England. The compilers of the report had clearly intended to have pictures added and there were at least two large blanks on each page. So all I had were these captions, in exactly these words:

> *Look! How nice dress these two street girls are wearing!*
> *Can a street girl wear such a nice dress?*
> *Or are they really street girl?*

The answer:

> *They are really street girls.*
> *A street girl specially a girl can't wear such a nice dress.*

'Can you just explain the significance of the "nice dress"?'

It seemed rather a silly question in the light of the stream of statistical information which had flowed over us so far, but it was all I could think of.

'Oh yes! Yes! Come! Come with us!'

We watched in amazement as she shoved her precious fact files carelessly away and stood up. She seemed transfigured by sheer excitement. Her supervisor, Mildred Monorama, was also radiant. Taken by surprise as we had been many times on our trip by the transformation of workers from po-faced lecturers into passionate disciples, I reflected on how sad it was that staff everywhere seemed to believe that only the driest factual breakdown of aims, objectives and financial distribution would impress visitors. But then, of course, we weren't here to check on exactly how the money had been spent and to evaluate the benefits experienced by every child in order to report back to governments or sponsors.

We scrambled to our feet and followed this little bundle of dynamite down the dark corridor. As she opened the door to a room full of shiny clean, beautifully dressed little girls, I found myself mentally echoing the strangely phrased question set out in the report:

Are they really street girl?

Remember we had just walked through the type of street scene which was becoming all too familiar. Small children breaking up bricks, carrying bundles, and grubbing through filthy piles of rubbish. These little ones are known as *tokias*, rag pickers, scavengers, urchins. They are not called children. They are not considered part of the future of the nation. They dig deep into the rotting refuse to find paper, metal, cardboard, bones, wood scraps, broken bricks, in fact anything that can be sold to the *mohajons*, the dealers, for a few taka a kilo. Many of them have mouth ulcers and running sores. All of them have tangled, filthy hair and grubby faces. Of course they have. How could these pathetic scraps of humanity possibly keep themselves clean?

'What we want is that these little girls learn to value themselves,' explained our host, 'so the question we asked ourselves was, how can we achieve this? How can we increase their sense of self-worth when no one else respects them? How can they experience self-respect when they smell horrible and they feel nasty, and when they see how different they are from the richer folk who pass them by in rickshaws?

'So we decided on the nice dress. When they come to us each morning they are wearing their own clothes. They wash and comb their hair and change into one of our clean dresses. They feel nice. They feel pretty. They look at each other and feel happy. They too are special. They too are children. And it is in this good mood that they go to their lessons and play their games and learn to sew and eat their tiffin and sing their songs.'

But what happens at the end of the afternoon?

'Then they change into their own clothes and go back to the streets.'

'But ...'

'I know that you think this is not good. Poor children going back into their dirty rags. But their nice dress would be sold or stolen. And the next day they will come again, and the next, and they will begin to want to be clean and to like the feeling of smelling good, and when they get older, about eleven, they will want to learn a trade so that they can continue to wear a nice dress, and because they will have a value for themselves they will think they do not want to be a prostitute.'

So simple. So clever. So Christlike.

Girl-child ghosts

A: 'What do you think you'll remember most about Bangladesh?'

Bridget and I asked each other that question again and again in the course of our trip. I suppose there is a sense in which it should be difficult to answer. Impressions and images have thronged our minds every day like the traffic of Dhaka itself, each one pushing and shoving and manoeuvring to take its place at the front of our consciousness. An abundance of people and places, conversations and faces continue to provide us with a rich harvest of recollections. We have witnessed everything from the darkness of despair to the bright inspiring colours of survival. I think you will be able to tell from the way we write about it, that the joy of our meeting with Shahnaj will live with us for ever. Apart from that absolutely central event, though, the experience that Bridget has just written about haunts us more than any other, I suppose because it was so terrible and so wonderful.

It was the problem that was terrible, and the ongoing solution that was wonderful.

The problem is one shared by most third world countries. Bangladesh as a whole is a desperately poor country with the majority of its inhabitants existing below the poverty line. In a place like Dhaka, the capital, where forty per cent of city dwellers live in the slums, and, generally speaking, women are still regarded as lesser beings, the plight of homeless girl children is nothing less than a major tragedy. Believe me, you do not want to know some of the facts that follow unless you are also willing to do something that will help to change them.

There are approximately one million street girls in Bangladesh, and a significant proportion of these live in Dhaka. Reading through the various reports available and speaking to workers on the project we were able to identify six groups of working children, but I expect there are lots of others.

1 Collectors of waste paper and other materials from streets, dustbins and garbage dumps. We saw these children everywhere we went, trying, in the foulest of conditions, to earn enough to eat on that particular day.
2 Sellers of flowers, drinking water, peanuts, betel leaves, cigarettes and other small items.
3 Carriers of lunch or 'tiffin' boxes to offices and other working places.
4 Brick or stone chippers.
5 Domestic servants.
6 Commercial sex workers. This oddly functional term for young prostitutes is one that has been adopted among those working on the project that we visited, and it accurately reflects the fact that morality comes a long way down the list of priorities for a young girl who has the hard facts of starvation and bleak homelessness staring her in the face. Prostitution starts very early for some of these girls.

It will be as sickening for you to read these words as it is for me to write them, but we were told of one child who was selling her body at the age of six. She died when she was eight from venereal disease. I wonder if that little scrap knew the four spiritual laws. I wonder if she had made a commitment. I wonder how she felt about the paradox of predestination and free will. I wonder if she went to heaven. If she did not, do you think that the Good Shepherd himself could have borne to live there for one more eternal day until he had searched frantically through the whole of hell and found her at last scratching around the infernal ash-heap on which she had assumed she must belong forever, and lifted her gently on to his shoulder and carried her home?

Many of the girl children on this list will be living on the street, often, as we witnessed for ourselves in the course of our journeys, near to railway and bus stations, earning their pittance of a wage in unhealthy, risky work environments, and receiving no education at all. In times of sickness they are likely to be alone and uncared for, and they will be continually vulnerable to sexual, mental, physical and financial exploitation.

The World Vision Dhaka street girl project began in 1997 with the express purpose of at least attempting to address these problems. The project has established a drop-in centre and an outreach centre, and it is in these places that we found the word 'wonderful' so applicable to the work that was being done.

We were met and shown around by project co-ordinators Mildred Monorama Anwar and Lufte Tahera, who, as Bridget says, eventually revealed themselves to be two human dynamos. Their zest and determination was fuelled by pure passion for the work they are doing. These two ladies mean business.

They explained that from Monday to Friday the commercial sex workers attend the centre from nine o'clock in the morning until four o'clock in the afternoon, the timetable being as follows:

9.00–2.30 : Taking a bath, preparing lunch for themselves and resting
2.30–3.00 : Attending non-formal education classes
3.00–4.30 : Counselling or education.

The latter period covers such areas as primary health care, reproductive health, and the risk factors involved in their own lives. It will also usually include recreation or games of some kind. One of the problems that workers continually face both with the commercial sex workers and with girls involved in other work on the street is that many of them have no real sense of what is 'normal'.

It is not easy for most of us because we are so rich, but try to imagine it.

You have lived without shelter on the streets for most of your short life. You probably have lip ulcers on both sides of your mouth because of the filthy conditions in which you live and work. You are generally dirty and smelly and badly dressed and you barely know how to clean yourself. You have never known what it means to be consistently loved and cared for. You have frequently been used and discarded for a few taka by men who regard you as little more than an inanimate object, a sort of mucky doll. You have spent each day of your life wondering if you will eat, wondering whether you will still be alive when night falls, and sometimes hoping that you will not.

For many of the girls who come to the centre these things are 'normal', and, very understandably, they take a lot of persuading that there could be some other way of life that is a genuine option for them. Girls who have been visiting the centre for more than a year are given lessons and counselling in these valuable areas:

Trust your own feelings and conscience, these are more important than what others say.
What are good feelings and bad feelings?
If someone's behaviour towards you is something you are not used to, you must take any measures necessary to ensure your safety, as every girl has the right to protect herself.
Children are precious, important and intelligent.
Some secrets may be safe, for instance, a birthday gift, but a child must understand where innocent fun and secrets end and something bad begins to happen.
Good touch and bad touch.
Current issues concerning girl children and women, such as rape, abuse or trafficking.
Girls' rights.
Effects of early marriage.
Where are my boundaries in all the different places that I find myself during the day?

As well as all these areas that are automatically discussed and taught in so many ordinary homes in this country, it is constantly stressed that education is important for all, and that it can be started at any time and any age. The girls are also aware that they are free to come and discuss whatever worries they have with the staff, who will try to discover ways to solve or reduce their problems. They are encouraged to stay as smart and clean as possible for the sake of their own health and self-image, and to believe that the project workers really are there to help them. On the practical side, and to help with the provision of increased income through safe means, embroidery and sewing, and the making of small paper bags for sale is taught on a regular basis at the centre.

So many case stories have been recorded. Here are just two of them, chosen at random. Ayesha is a tiny seven-year-old girl who sleeps on the road under the sky. Project workers found her in August 1997, in ward number 31 of Dhaka city. She sells water near the Kamalapur railway and bus station. She does not go to school. She cannot read or write. She has two younger siblings and has to care for them as well as helping her mother, who is one of the stream of people arriving in the city looking for work. Ayesha does not think it is a good idea to study because 'Mother has no money, and I have no time. There is no need to go to school.' She lives, surrounded by filth and rubbish, under the railway bridge near Kamalapur station.

Sukhi is twelve years old and her work is carrying lunch containers to people who work in offices. She carries four of these tiffin boxes each day for four people who work in the Notijheel area. She lives with her older sister near the railway in ward 31. There was another sister who was just a little older than her, but this girl died of rheumatic fever with complications. Sukhi is the most intelligent and obedient student in the non-formal education class at the centre. She is now in grade three, and she came first in her exam.

Sukhi comes regularly to the centre for education, recreation and embroidery work. She appears at nine o'clock in the morning, goes to do her work at noon, then returns to the centre at three o'clock. Soon after she began to attend, workers discovered that Sukhi had been suffering from rheumatic fever since her childhood, and was already receiving treatment at the rheumatic department of Sohrowardi Hospital. World Vision workers collected her records from the hospital in March 1998, and since then the project has been providing all her medical expenses.

Secret boxes

B: Sadly, we never actually met the prostitutes. They had been there in the morning but were now back at work. We were shown the room where they spent time together each day, the place where they washed their clothes and changed after having a bath and talked and made friends and ate their lunch together.

There was nothing in the room, at least, nothing of immediate interest, nothing except a pile of large boxes, each with a lock.

'What are these for?'

'Oh, these are where they keep their things. They have no home, you see. Nowhere that is their own. They can put their things in here and know they are safe. Each girl has her own key to her own box. It is important to them.'

Important. I should jolly well think it is. A locked place that is your very own. A private place. A place that no one can invade. A place no one can take possession of against your will. A place that is yours to open and share only when you decide to, and only with those you choose. A place to keep secret – a part of yourself. For these used, abused children, I bet it's important.

Did we do well enough?

A: At the end of the afternoon we were ushered through to a large room where we found the younger group of girls sitting in neat rows, waiting to put a show on for us. Sitting down cross-legged on the floor at the back of the room, we smiled encouragingly in response to excited grins on thirty or so faces as the girls peeped back quickly over their shoulders to check that we were settled and ready for the performance to start. We were ready. They began.

The different acts that we saw reflected some of the activities that groups regularly engaged in at the centre. One of the bigger girls played the part of a maid, exhausted and discouraged by being made to work too hard by her mistress, an acting performance of genuine concentration and power. A younger child, tough but vulnerable, with the screwed-up eyes and tense features of a kid who had been struggling to march uphill against the harsh winds of suffering all through her life, sang a solo for us, accompanied by one of the workers on that wonderful instrument, the Bangladeshi harmonium. Her voice was strong and clear. It may have lacked mellowness, but it was bravely confident and perfectly in tune. Something about the uncompromising nature of it got right down into the very roots of my soul. It was so bold and so redolent of survival against the odds. I wish you could have heard the way in which that small survivor lifted up her head and sang out with every ounce of her being.

Then there was the community singing. We had already heard one group's rendition of 'We Shall Overcome' on another occasion. It had been immensely moving. Somehow, in this very special context, the optimistic words of this freedom song, one that had been a familiar part of our sixties childhood, and the unquenchable singing of children locked in the chains of poverty and neglect, were filled with an almost unbearable pathos.

Overcome?

Did these children really believe that they would overcome? How? How would they overcome? Had seven or eight or nine or ten or eleven years of being considered next to valueless not convinced them that their chances of overcoming were virtually nil? I looked around at them with their newly washed hair, sitting in their neat rows in their clean dresses, enjoying their fragile, temporary sense of well-being, and my spirit rocked with grief at the thought that millions of children like these are forced to struggle desperately through sadly unrepeatable years of their lives when they should be playing and laughing and being cuddled and always having someone safe to run to. But I also thanked God that this particular group of little lost people had at least met the love of Jesus in the form of these two ladies and the other workers in the project.

And what on earth did the street girls make of it all, I wondered?

'These people in this project thing,' they must have said to themselves, 'are not part of our families, nor did they know us until we came here. They ask nothing in return for all they do, other than our willingness to help in making our own lives better. Why do they care? Who sent them ...?'

The final verse of the song was sung in English, specially for us, I expect.

We are not alone
We are not alone
We are not alone today
O-oh, deep in my heart, I do believe
That we are not alone today ...

The song ended and the girls were asked if they had any questions for us.

'Yes,' said one little girl, standing up ramrod straight and addressing us through a translator, 'did we do well enough?'

Silence for a moment.

'Well enough?'

'Did we do well enough for more money to come so that the project will not have to stop in October?'

I suspect that if I had been in possession of the necessary hundred and fifty thousand pounds at that precise moment I would have written a cheque and handed it over. The little girl was absolutely right, we learned later. The project, clearly not a self-sustainable one by its very nature, was due to finish in the coming autumn. Unless new funds appeared from somewhere, perhaps through World Vision adopting the project as part of an area development, there would be nowhere for these children and others like them to take refuge from the grim, grimmer and grimmest realities of their lives.

How would you have answered that child's question?

'Of *course* you've done well enough,' we said, 'of course you have.'

But all we could realistically promise was that we would tell anyone who would listen about their problem, and, by and large, we have done that. We have, for instance, told you.

Those kids sang out lustily and confidently that they are not alone. I pray to God they are right.

• THE LAST DAY •

Eating out

A: Before leaving for Bangladesh we had already discovered that almost all of the so-called 'Indian' restaurants in Great Britain are run and staffed by folk from Bangladesh. The fact that we were long-term devotees of this kind of cuisine gave – if you will excuse the expression – a little extra spice to our trip. Just as I had enjoyed my first authentically Irish pint of Guinness at a pub near Cork in 1998, so I was now going to sample Bangladeshi food in its true place of origin in the year 2000.

Honesty compels me to admit that the experience turned out to be a variable one. Eating at our own hotel and in the restaurants nearby was extremely pleasant (not counting the staring red mullet, which wasn't their fault), but there were one or two occasions when I felt I was taking my life in my hands, or rather, in my stomach. There was the restaurant in one large town, for instance, which was so dark inside that it was almost impossible to see the food on our plates. No,

I am not talking about dimmed lights, romantic or otherwise. I am talking about the kind of power-cut darkness that means you have to peer at the face of the person next to you to find out who it is, and in which your fork can only be found by fumbling blindly around the surface of the tablecloth with one nervous hand.

This in itself might not have mattered, but the waiters in this particular establishment had a habit of clearing their throats in a horribly thorough and committed sort of way, then spitting equally loudly just before coming out of the kitchen holding little bowls of something you couldn't quite identify because it was too dark.

It put you off a bit.

Whenever we were guests we always ate well, if rather frequently. There were days when we visited quite a number of different groups and projects, and because etiquette clearly demanded that guests should always be offered food and drink of some kind before getting down to business, those days could begin to seem like one long meal, accompanied by endless cups of tea – with sugar. It was nice, but filling.

On our last night before returning home, without any escort at all for once, Bridget and I, searching for somewhere to eat, walked around the corner from our hotel and found ourselves passing a restaurant called the Thirteen Coins, which we had never visited before. We went in. As usual there appeared to be no less than seven staff to each customer, but that didn't matter. The menu! Ah, the menu! Steak and chips, and things like that, beautifully cooked and incredibly cheap. As we strolled contentedly home a couple of hours later we reflected on the fact that we always have done things – and probably always will – in exactly the same way. We had found a restaurant just round the corner that suited us down to the ground, but we had found it by accident, on the last day.

Oh, Calcutta!

B: Here we were for the last time perched on the blue cover of the double bed in the Begum home, Shahnaj tucked comfortably between us, with the baby trying yet again to teethe on my necklace and Simon and Ragip trying yet again to stop her.

Adrian was looking absolutely exhausted, and I was very aware of how the last few days had taken the stuffing out of him after his nasty illness. Even worse, it was photocall as usual, and I knew that it was going to take a miracle to get any more smiles from him. I sensed rather than saw Shahnaj glance upwards at her new, big friend's weary face. Then, with a slight wiggle and a little giggle she put up both hands and pulled his face down until her mouth was level with his ear.

'Calcutta! Calcutta!' she whispered.

The first time she had heard Adrian pronounce the name of the Indian city 'Calcutta' during our theatre trip, his mispronunciation had amused her enormously, and she had been at great pains to correct him. She had also teased him by repeating it every few minutes on the journey back. Now she was intent on cheering him up, and what better way than to tease him out of his misery. Of course, she succeeded, and for a moment it could have been Kate sitting between us, Kate, the arch-professional in restoring her daddy's good humour by just the same method.

I thought of Shahnaj's father somewhere out there on his rickshaw and smiled. He didn't stand a chance! She'd wrap him round her little finger for a good few years yet.

As we said a very sad goodbye to these lovely children and their adorable baby cousin, I was already aware that my abiding memory of them would be of their warmth, and their intuitive loving concern, not just for each other, but also for their funny big visitors from another world.

Bangladeshi baby

***A:** Little baby Bangladesh*
Bursting with your Bangla, Belgian, British, Bantu babiness
You flatter me
You babies always do
By nestling to my chest
And in your eyes, Bangla baby, in those dark and dusky pools,
I see that you know all you need to know for now
And we who think we know much more are fools

For sadly all our wisdom offers for your future
Is much less than you will need
Little baby Bangladesh
Clutching at my collar with your tiny boxing Bangla fists
Please let me say a prayer for you
A supplication on your infant head
I hope your baby legs grow strong
Walk well upon these dusty streets
And find each day your daily bread
God grant a love that fills your heart, a life that will be long
May you be loved, and blessed with friends, and often kissed,
and free
And Bangla baby that will be enough
I do not ask that you remember me

Parting

A: Shahnaj was in floods of tears when we finally said goodbye to her. So overcome was she that she had to retreat into the privacy of her father's rickshaw. Her mother and sister were crying as well. I don't know if they could all see how near to tears Bridget and I were.

This often happens when these children part from their sponsors, we were told.

Oh, well, that's all right then, isn't it? In that case it doesn't matter nearly so much, does it?

What are we doing?

B: 'Are you sure we're not just creating dependency by pouring money into an area like this? Are we not in danger of taking away their dignity? I mean, surely if they really wanted to they could pull out all the stops – climb out of the poverty trap themselves. Oh, I don't know, it's just that I work hard for my money – it's not that I mind giving. I just want to be sure that it's going to the right people.'

As Dhiman drives us for the last time through the streets of Dhaka on our way to the airport, we are both rather quiet, our hearts and minds full to the brim with all that we have seen and heard and thought and felt. Suddenly I remember that question. Was it really only a fortnight ago that I had that conversation with a member of our church? It had been an interesting experience telling people what we were going to be doing in Bangladesh. It seemed to bring to the surface many people's feelings about projects such as the ones we were going out to see, and we had been surprised by how many had only the vaguest notion of what World Vision is and what it does. Others, like this anxious lady, who expressed her views to me at coffee-time after the service, were clearly uneasy about what they saw as patronizing interference in the lives of folk who should be encouraged to stand on their own two feet.

So, does child sponsorship spring the poverty trap for those families who benefit from the scheme? Does it help to set them free, or does it simply create a new problem of dependency, sapping the dignity of those who receive aid? Do I really know? Of course not after such a short time, but maybe I have been given an inkling.

The very expression 'poverty trap' suggests a victim caught by the strong claws of a device designed to maim and capture. The victim struggles constantly in order to escape, but eventually, bleeding and exhausted, energy spent, gives in, gives up and dies in agony. Poverty as we had seen it over the last two weeks was clearly just such a trap for many. Everywhere we saw the struggling innocent, and occasionally, in the very poorest, we saw the dulled, stony eyes of the defeated. But what epitomized our limited experience was the amazing fight that these brave people were putting up in order to survive.

I remembered an article I had read only the day before in a copy of the *Dhaka Guardian* delivered to our hotel room. It was written by Syed Badrul Ahsan, a journalist who has been resident in Britain for three years but who has made the decision that the time has come to go back to his homeland, Bangladesh. He talks about how every twilight his thoughts have been drawn back to the old country:

> *I have remained in contact with the thin man who plies his rickshaw day after day to keep his children alive. And I have remembered the weatherbeaten faces which have looked into my face every time I have walked out of a shop loaded with delicacies for*

home. These are my people. They have struggled all their lives for survival, all their dignity lost in the strenuousness of that struggle.'

All their dignity lost, all their hope gone.

As I finished reading it I had thought of Shahnaj's father and the dark shadows of exhaustion upon his thin face. For five years his daughter had received our support through sponsorship. What had that meant in real terms? Was he now living a life of dependent ease, secure in the knowledge that all his needs and those of his family were being met? Was he heck as like!!

Conversations with his family and with World Vision staff had made it clear that he, like most fathers of sponsored children, works his fingers to the bone in order to provide for his family. Seven days a week, every week, every year he drives a motorized rickshaw through the polluted streets of old Dhaka. It costs him 200 taka in rent a day. He takes 300 taka a day, which means that his take-home pay for a long, exhausting day's work is one pound. The first time I heard just how paltry the average wages are for many of the menial jobs on the streets of the city I was so horrified that I think I felt the need to rationalize the situation.

Of course, I conjectured hopefully, one pound is worth far more in Bangladesh than it is here in the UK.

Absolutely right. In Bangladesh we found that one pound has the spending power of about five pounds over here. So that's much better, isn't it? It makes us feel more comfortable to think of him having five pounds a day to sustain six people in his family including two teenagers and two growing children. That, of course, is assuming he is never sick, because he will still have to pay his 200 taka daily rent whether he goes out in his rickshaw or not, quite apart from any medical costs incurred by his illness. Rent for their house, 200 taka a week, will have to come out of his earnings, as well as school fees for the other children, repairs to the home and care for any elderly members of the family who receive hardly anything from the state. And all that is before you think about food and clothes!

No wonder few of the children we met in the slums or in the poorest rural communities had the opportunity to experience the fulfilment of education. Few had ever experienced the fulfilment of sufficient rice to fill their tummies.

No wonder there hasn't been much room in most of these fathers' heads for hopes and dreams about their future, or that of their children. The fight for sheer survival occupies every waking hour as they steer their passengers through the traffic maze of the cities or break their backs in the paddy fields.

So, in the face of all this, what has our sponsorship of Shahnaj actually achieved? Well, as I looked into her parents' eyes when we said goodbye – and I say this with awe because I can hardly believe it is true – I saw those very flames of hope.

Hope, partly because the money has meant that at least one beloved child's education is secure.

Hope because of the secondary effects on all of them, like Simon's tailoring course, and the health of the whole family.

But also because it has kept alive this spark, this belief that they matter to someone, a reason to go on fighting, and to hope that one day maybe, just maybe, they will not only survive, but perhaps even overcome.

Going home

A: We caught our plane for home. Droning through the eternal night towards England, I said, 'Bridget, that was the third world, right?'

'Right.'

'We're heading for the first world, right?'

'Right.'

Pause.

'What's the second world?'

'Dunno,' said Bridget sleepily, 'don't care. Should only be one silly world. More sponsors. More lives changed. Goodnight ...'

I sighed and wriggled in my seat. Fat chance (literally) of me getting much sleep in this springloaded clamp of a so-called seat. Must lose some weight. Really must. Soon as I got home I'd go up the gym and really – you know – get on with it. We'd see Kate and David and Joe soon. That would be nice. Already Bangladesh was beginning to seem like a strange dream – a really strange dream ...

I fell asleep. Somewhere, far below in the slums of Dhaka, a little girl was dreaming her future.

• CONCLUSION •

A: Three things strike me as I sit here, a photograph of Shahnaj propped in front of me, reflecting on this trip of ours.

The first is about evangelism. Before I went to Bangladesh there were a lot of questions heaving restlessly around inside me about the business of providing practical help, but not actually preaching the gospel in words, as it were. A recent exchange during a car journey with a friend who is an elder at one of our local churches may indicate the direction in which my thinking has moved since then.

'We had an elders' meeting last night,' he said, 'and among other things we discussed that woman who was in the local paper recently – you know, quite young, the one who lost all her family in a car crash. We thought it would be nice to send her some flowers, but we weren't sure what to put on the card with them. I mean – she's not a church-goer or anything, so it's a bit difficult to get it right. Know what I mean?'

'Mmm, yes, difficult.'

'What would you put?'

I stared at the road ahead and thought for a moment. I knew what he was getting at. Some of those elders would undoubtedly be seeing this flower-sending exercise as one of those occasions referred to rather gruesomely in church circles as 'an opportunity for outreach'. In my mind I returned to the streets of Dhaka for a moment or two. I saw need, colour, eyes, despair and hope.

'Why not send them anonymously?' I suggested. 'Why not just be Jesus instead of talking about him? Maybe God will use the flowers better than your group of elders ever could.'

My friend laughed and shook his head. 'You could well be right,' he said, 'but I honestly can't see one or two of them going for that, I honestly can't ...'

In a country like Bangladesh, World Vision workers cannot evangelize in the formal sense, but make no mistake about it, they, and the other aid agencies, are Jesus walking the streets and the slums and the rural areas.

'World Vision loves us,' said the woman in the savings group.

'The work of World Vision forms a bridge that I can cross to reach the people,' said the priest.

If Jesus is there – and I can assure you that, in the hands and feet of his servants, he is – do bear in mind that he has quite a good record when it comes to evangelism. Trust him.

The second reflection is, I suppose, linked to the first, and I find it rather frighteningly stark. The fact is that, if we Christians are not active in the sort of places that we visited, nor, as far as I can tell, is God. Children starve and are abused and die on rubbish heaps. God doesn't send angels to save them, or if he does, it doesn't happen very often. I am sorry if that offends you, but if it does, tell me how it is not true. Here in this country we are so rich that we can indulge in the luxury of spending hour after religious hour on spiritual navel-gazing. I know – I've done it. We get away with murder, don't we?

Part of me wishes that I had never seen the slums of Dhaka, because I know now that Jesus is out there, not just in the form of his followers, but, as Mother Teresa always insisted, in the wasted bodies and hopeless eyes of people who do not know what it means to be properly fed, let alone loved. Part of me, though, is glad to have seen those sights, because it enables me to pass on these thoughts with a passion that would have been impossible a few months ago.

My third reflection is about that bit in Genesis where we are told that we are made in the image of God. Meeting Shahnaj and her family strongly reinforced that particular truth. Where love and care, those crucial seeds ultimately planted only by God, are feeding the roots of any situation, you will see the same fruits whether you are in the midst of enormous wealth or abject poverty. It is shocking to see what the slums do to people, but it is equally amazing to see what they do *not* do to others.

And finally ...

A few days after getting back from Bangladesh we took one of Sanjay's superb portrait photographs of Shahnaj along to a shop in town and had it colour photocopied to A4 size, and then laminated so that fingermarks could be cleaned off (everything in our house seems to undergo so much *handling*). That's the one that's in front of me now as I write. It really is a beautiful picture. Shahnaj has at last managed to sneak that velvet jacket in front of the camera, and if her smile got much wider it would disappear round the back of her head.

When I look into her eyes, though, it seems to me two emotions are visible. One is a simple joy in living, particularly marked in this youngster, but, as I have just indicated, far from uncommon in eleven-year-olds who are loved and wanted, however rich or poor they may be. The other is a worry or a question or perhaps even the slightest shadow of foreboding.

You are not allowed to be a child in the slums for very long.

One of the last things Shahnaj expressed through a translator before we left was a wish that we could whisk her off with us in the aeroplane back to our house in England. We laughed this off, of course, as one does – must, but every time I look at her picture those words come back to me, and I wonder what her future will actually be. That simply expressed wish, a fragile butterfly of a thought, attractive and short-lived, has become a symbol of the responsibility that has been laid on Bridget and me to bring the poor of that distant country back to Great Britain in our hearts so that they may indeed live with us here and become known to others. And so, by the grace of God, they will.

But I have to conclude by saying that, for Bridget and me, something has changed for ever. For us, as well as the symbol, there is a person. Pray that God will allow us to see Shahnaj again one day.

The world is full of children and communities who need a little help. If you would like to sponsor a child yourself, do get in touch with our friends at World Vision. God bless you, and thanks for reading this book.